Orchestrating School Change
Transforming Your Leadership

Author
Michael Murphy, Ed.D.
Foreword
Stephanie Hirsh, Ph.D.

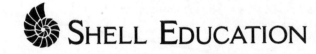

SHELL EDUCATION

Shell Education

5301 Oceanus Drive
Huntington Beach, CA 92649-1030
http://www.shelleducation.com

ISBN 978-1-4258-1315-4

© 2014 Shell Educational Publishing, Inc.

Orchestrating
School Change
Transforming
Your
Leadership

Table of Contents

Foreword

I have worked alongside Mike Murphy facilitating school plans in more than 50 schools. When we first began this work, we knew the process inside and out, and had great expectations for those plans. While some changes ultimately prevailed, too few of those changes can be attributed to the plans we helped educators put on paper.

It took me many more experiences to understand at a deeper level how to facilitate change to produce desired outcomes for educators and students. I remain more of a student—Mike is the real practitioner. Readers are so fortunate that Mike is sharing his secrets as a masterful change facilitator. For those who have wondered what it takes to finally make change stick, *Orchestrating School Change: Transforming Your Leadership* will be like music to your ears.

There is an art as well as a discipline attached to successful change initiatives, and Mike understands both deeply. This is why the metaphor of an orchestra is so powerful for exploring this process. Mike writes about the "orchestration" of leading school improvement. He refers to the fact that orchestration requires a maestro, someone who is an artist of considerable skill. "This maestro must demonstrate artistry in choreographing the complexities of a major initiative and designing supportive efforts to keep the initiative alive and thriving as a communal effort. The maestro must, at the same time, show great skill in masterminding the day-to-day efforts to spotlight progress and improvement of all of the stakeholders of this improvement community. These two ideas are central to orchestrating change in schools."

Attending to the capacity of his players to achieve the changes they desire is embedded throughout Mike's orchestration process. He realizes that without effective professional learning, the maestro can't count on his or her staff to play the complex passages in front of them or ultimately achieve their desired outcomes for students.

I particularly appreciate Mike's acknowledgement of the importance of the maestro's relationships and conversations with the educators in his systems. He sees that a maestro must be able to establish and sustain a vision, offer meaningful feedback to educators at wildly different skill and readiness levels, and facilitate interactions large and small. The leader who hopes to pull that off has his or her own needs for learning and support, and this book goes a long way towards building a helpful score for the future maestro. I know that the skills I have developed, and my understanding of what makes change stick, were certainly enhanced through the work I did with Mike and what I see happening in the field each day in schools and school systems that implement the kinds of strategies he writes about in this valuable resource.

—Stephanie Hirsh, Ph.D.
Executive Director
Learning Forward

Today's new and veteran school leaders are responsible for navigating the move to a 21st century learning environment...no small task. Michael Murphy's Orchestrating School Change provides them with a wonderful balance of theory and practice around the school change process and when and why change initiatives take hold. The case studies, sample templates, and resources are both practical and ready-to-use.

—Annette V. Alpern, M.Ed., M.S., Ed.D.
Deputy Superintendent, Educational Services
Redondo Beach Unified School District
Redondo Beach, California

Acknowledgements

This work is a culmination of many years of practice, learning, and numerous "splendid openings" that my colleagues and mentors have afforded me. So, to them, I am deeply grateful.

First, to my supervisors, mentors, and colleagues who have led my learning along the way. I'm so appreciative of your patience, creativity, and "smarts." Special thanks to Dr. Terry Crane, Dr. Betty Ann Fults, Bill Branum, Dr. Mike Moses, Dr. Carol Tomlinson, Dr. Frank Kemerer, Dr. Gerald Ponder, Dr. Stephanie Hirsh, Dr. Shirley Hord, Sonia Caus Gleason, Glenn Singleton, and Rick Smith.

I am so appreciative of my colleagues (really, you're much more than that!) who have witnessed this work with me along the way. They include Robbie Mitchell, Dr. Vicki Kirk, Dr. Adele Bovard, Linda Sykut, all of my colleagues at Learning Forward, and the team from Round Rock ISD (Texas).

Thanks to Corinne Burton at Shell Education for her insights and strategic guidance of such quality materials to help practitioners orchestrate a masterful job. A special thanks to my editor, Wendy Conklin, for her "take no prisoners" attitude, yet gentle patience and guidance.

Lastly, as always, a special wink and thanks to my family and pals for understanding my passion for the work and giving me the encouragement and space to make my work so meaningful.

What Is School Orchestration, and Why Is It So Important?

As leaders, we are all focused on initiating, supporting, and maintaining effective changes in our schools to serve students in better ways. This book serves as your guide for making those kinds of significant and much-needed changes happen. As we begin our look into this kind of change, consider this all too common example of traditional change efforts:

Culver Elementary School: A Case Study

T.M. Culver Elementary School, a K–5 school with approximately 600 students in a suburban/urban part of the Midwest, boasts a relatively diverse population. Between 30–40 percent of students in Culver do not meet the state proficiencies in reading and writing, and a significant area of concern has been in mathematics. Culver's students, across all grade levels, do generally worse in mathematics than other students in similar elementary schools in the region.

The culture at Culver is relatively stable. The grade-level teams at Culver have always met regularly to discuss curriculum, instruction, and student discipline issues. Trust and congeniality seem to be high within, and among, the grade levels at Culver. Teachers enjoy friendly professional and personal relationships with each other, and turnover among the staff at Culver is relatively low.

Culver's principal, Shirley Russell, has been at Culver for seven years, and she has become increasingly concerned about overall student performance in reading, writing, and especially mathematics. A few years ago, she directed her teachers to analyze the student performance data and meet in teams to address the performance gaps. These efforts have continued for several years, but Culver still has not met its targeted performance standards in mathematics. While they met their targets in reading and writing, Ms. Russell was still concerned that many students were not as successful as they could be in those areas either.

For one full year, Ms. Russell gathered data to illustrate her concern, with the hope that the data would also point to remedies. In order to help her clarify the problem, she spent large amounts of time in teachers' classrooms. She conducted informal walk-through observations and required formal teacher observations. A pattern in these observations began to emerge. Ms. Russell noticed that in the vast majority of cases, teachers were teaching to the whole group, even in reading. She rarely saw the teachers involve the students in conversations about their learning. Most of the teaching was "stand and deliver" by the teacher, and this information concerned her. She knew that with the move toward more intense learning standards, required by the state, the focus had to be on differentiating the work and engaging the students in longer, more sophisticated analyses of learning and application of skills. She knew that the "stand and deliver" approach to teaching would not address the intent of these new learning standards.

At the end of her year of classroom visits and analysis, Shirley Russell discussed her concerns with her leadership team, which consisted of grade-level representatives and special-area representatives. In these discussions, she mentioned what she was seeing in the classrooms and why different teaching strategies might address their student performance needs better.

This series of discussions with her leadership team culminated in the decision that professional development in differentiation strategies might address the concerns about whole-class teaching, and the lack of grouping and altering of work or processes to meet individual needs.

The leadership team agreed to study differentiation on their own for several months. Principal Russell sent two members of the team to a seminar on differentiation. In addition, the team began a book study on differentiation and met twice a month to discuss their readings, learning, and ideas for Culver.

At the end of this period of study, Ms. Russell's leadership team conveyed general enthusiasm for the extensive professional development in differentiation for the faculty. It was determined, by the team, that this professional development would begin in August of the upcoming school year. Principal Russell, excited that her team had come to this conclusion, jumped at the chance to begin initiating this professional development at her school.

Principal Russell knew that if she were to undertake this major initiative, her central office would need to be supportive. She met with key central office leaders and illustrated her concerns. The central office staff members were enthusiastic about the professional development and offered a small amount of funds to support the initial training.

The leadership team began the August training with an overview that lasted one-half day. Following this overview, two consultants, nationally known for their expertise in differentiation, conducted the training with the staff. This training lasted an additional two days. At the end of the training, Ms. Russell asked participants to complete a "ticket out the door." This informal evaluation revealed favorable responses to the training and general enthusiasm for the ideas presented in the training.

Once the school year began, Ms. Russell began supporting the implementation of differentiation in small steps or low-prep strategies. She assumed that because she had discussed the idea so thoroughly with her leadership team, all teachers understood the goals of the training. Russell pressed for implementation of low-prep strategies by communicating directly with teachers in informal conversations. She sought opportunities to troubleshoot the initiative with her staff and encouraged all reluctant or hesitant teachers to get on board with trying differentiated strategies. Almost all of the conversations Ms. Russell had with her teachers during September or October were generally positive and no real opposition was voiced. Principal Russell was thrilled and scheduled her November follow-up training.

The November differentiation training was conducted by the same two national consultants and lasted two additional days. At the end of the training, respondents were again asked to give their feedback. At that time, feedback was generally positive again. At the completion of the training, Ms. Russell announced that she would be in classrooms to support the implementation of differentiated strategies.

During November and December, classroom visits were conducted by Ms. Russell. As she visited classrooms, she began to notice the implementation of differentiated strategies was inconsistent. Some teachers were implementing only one or two strategies. Other teachers, however, were not seen implementing any visible differentiated practices. She was alarmed as the feedback from the training had been so generally positive. She decided to visit team meetings to support the implementation of the training. During these meetings, she reminded teachers of the practices they should be implementing. Again, during these meetings there was no overt opposition to the practices she was promoting.

By January of that year, Russell had not noticed remarkable improvement to the practices she had seen in September and October. In fact, it seemed that most teachers had adopted one or two differentiated strategies and were using them over and over, not pursuing any deeper exploration of sophisticated measures taught in the extensive training. In fact, Ms. Russell began to hear, for the first time, open resentment to the lack of involvement in the original decision as well as the changes that were being required of teachers. During team meetings with Ms. Russell, relationships seemed awkward and a bit strained. Principal Russell began targeting teachers who she thought were most oppositional to the practices and started to spend more time in their classrooms to send them the message that the changes were important. She was direct with these resistant teachers, requiring them to implement the differentiated strategies immediately. Principal Russell began documenting these teachers in writing and sending them to other teachers' classrooms to observe differentiated strategies. These efforts yielded few changes with the reluctant teachers' practices.

In addition, parent complaints began to emerge. Apparently, teachers were communicating to parents their dissatisfaction with the new instructional practices, stating that they were expected to do too much, there was not enough time to plan, and that students were confused about the new strategies. Parents began questioning the changes and openly questioned the intelligence of making such instructional changes. Principal Russell held firm with the intent of the differentiated practices professional development and asked the parents for patience as they made the changes.

What Happened at Culver Elementary?

Does this story seem familiar? This all too typical case requires us to consider these questions:

- Why was the change at Culver Elementary never fully actualized?

- What was going on in the culture of the school to be so resistant so quickly?

- What evidence did Ms. Russell have to assume things were going well?

- What evidence could she have collected to get a better feel for the changes?

- Why didn't the training result in actual ongoing implementation of the strategies?

- What support did the teachers need from Ms. Russell? What did they get?

Shirley Russell worked hard to implement differentiation at Culver Elementary School, and she had data to support the need. She followed what seemed to be a natural, seemingly logical path for leading the changes. Yet, in spite of her best efforts, this initiative fell flat as so many often do in our schools. She was never able to put together a system of support and responses to move the initiative forward, toward full, lasting implementation. Russell's orchestration resulted in more "noise" than lasting, balanced music. This example illustrates the need for a different kind of leadership—a maestro's orchestration of different elements, which together create a symphony of sustained improvement.

The word "orchestration" is meaningful to all of us who are dedicated to leading and facilitating school improvement. Central to the idea of orchestration is the concept of "masterminding"—the engineering, directing, arranging, and organizing of projects of significant merit. An artistic reading of the word reminds us that orchestration is highly correlated with the concept of "choreographing"—the conceiving, planning, and directing of a "dance" having multiple complex and synchronous components. If we take these ideas associated with the word *orchestration*, we learn much about our roles in nurturing, supporting, and demanding long-lasting change in our schools.

To be effective and efficient school leaders, we must view ourselves as orchestrating (masterminding and choreographing) improvement in our schools. Indeed, to orchestrate requires a maestro, someone who is an artist of considerable skill. This maestro must demonstrate artistry in choreographing the complexities of a major initiative and designing supportive efforts to keep the initiative alive and thriving as a communal effort. The maestro must, at the same time, show great skill in masterminding the day-to-day efforts to spotlight progress and improvement to all of the stakeholders in this community improvement. These two ideas are central to orchestrating change in schools. Therefore, if you find yourself in the middle of orchestrating numerous significant changes and critical initiatives for the benefit of students in your schools, this book is your resource. No matter the initiative, no matter the level—elementary, middle, or high school—any work, if it is worth doing, requires careful and thoughtful orchestration if it is to succeed.

Too many of our best school efforts fall apart during the first two years of implementation. This failure is not due to a lack of effort; rather, the failure is due to a lack of careful orchestration of efforts, balancing the press for change and the support for individual improvement, throughout the initiative's new life until it becomes embedded into the culture of the school.

Figure 1.1 Imbalance of the Press for Change

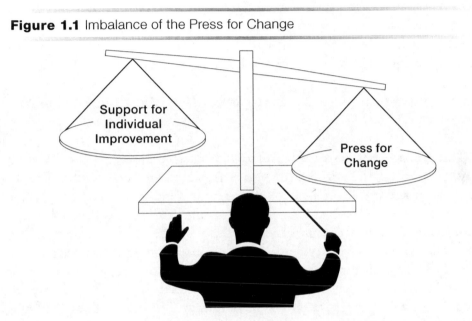

An imbalance of the press for change and the support for individual improvement actually creates disequilibrium at the school (see Figure 1.1). Thus usually sending the message that tremendous, exhausting effort will probably only occur at the beginning of the change and that the changes are temporary. The predictable exhaustion results, then, in an abandonment of effort. Simply put, the orchestration is too tiresome and the demands of practice unreasonable at first. Seeing no alternative set of strategies and understanding a long history of approaching change in this way, the smart folks simply walk away from it and wait cautiously and cynically for the next "great idea." Thus, our usual concert of school change is a short one, and the results are not met with thunderous applause.

While orchestration of change is complex, it *is* possible. Therefore, when considering or beginning any major change at a school, whether it be implementing new rigorous standards, creating differentiated classrooms, developing flexible scheduling for high school students such as modified blocks, or executing a balanced literacy design to rethink the teaching of reading at the elementary level, use this book to balance your efforts to orchestrate a full implementation of *your* initiative. Adapt the tools and frameworks in this book to provide evidence of the change. Practice the feedback frameworks to hold powerful and purposeful conversations about the change. Just as a maestro balances his or her approach to leading an orchestra, look at all of the instrumental work at the school and strategically facilitate the blending of your efforts throughout the concert of change.

Focus questions, notes, and measures for your orchestration of change include:

What Are the Fundamental Ideas We Need to Be Thinking About? Chapter Two begins with an overall graphic framework of the content and tools of the book, providing a foundation for the leader as he or she continues to use the book as a resource for lasting change. The chapter also details what we know about orchestration—the idea that masterminding these changes requires relationship-rich collaboration with teachers. Using this chapter as a springboard into their work, leaders learn that working in concert with teachers requires a differentiated approach built on an understanding of teachers as people as well as professionals. These "lessons of change" undergird orchestration and must be contemplated at the beginning and throughout the work.

What Will Make My Actions Effective? Chapter Three examines critical decisions the leader must make in becoming knowledgeable about the initiative. In essence, the chapter asks two questions. The first question is "What are the big ideas behind this initiative, and what content must I master in order to continue to orchestrate a support system to ensure that the work goes forward?" The second question is "How do I continue to work with teachers to orchestrate this initiative when they know more about it than I do?"

How Do I Develop a Vision for This Initiative? Chapter Four explores the power and necessity of having a vision for the change being sought. This vision is different in scope and direction from the customary "vision statements." A vision is needed for any initiative—a written picture or description of how things will be changed as a result of this particular work. This vision is vital if people are to be reminded of the moral purpose of the change as well as the progress they are making toward that vision. This chapter not only explores the rationale for the vision, but it also provides step-by-step processes for creating this vision for your initiative.

What Kinds of Conversations Should I Be Having about This Initiative? Chapter Five is all about the relationships built through the critical conversations leaders have with teachers every day. Central to this relationship is the idea of trust, how to build it and why it is so important when pressed for results. Leaders will also find the conversation frameworks and feedback strategies useful as they embed their daily management with these crucial, quick, and informal dialogues. This chapter also answers an important question, "How can I resist the urge to fix resistance and see resistance as constructive to my work?"

How Do I Develop Targeted Professional Development to Sustain the Initiative? Chapter Six is the maestro's guide for continuous adult learning. Designing powerful professional learning—informal and "just in time" to support the initiative—is essential to long-lasting results. Various designs and effective, inexpensive professional learning models enhance the maestro's "baton" for continuing development of knowledge and skills to translate the initiative into practice.

How Do I Know if Anything Is Changing as a Result of This Work? Chapter Seven focuses on results. Using tools and strategies from a variety of sources and two evaluative frameworks, the leader meets evaluation head on with data and information to see if implementation of learning is occurring in classrooms and if teachers are routinely using the strategies and adapting their strategies to get even better student results.

Can I See an Example of This in Action? Chapter Eight offers the school leader an opportunity to see how all of the work fits within a case study. Through this real-life example, the leader can reflect on the strategic decisions that were made and how the concepts, tools, and frameworks in this book all unite to achieve lasting change.

You are not alone in the work. The vast majority of our colleagues are devoted to students and want to succeed. Those highly skilled and dedicated educators have great potential for shared leadership in your ranks. Yet, just like the maestro of an orchestra, your staff members need someone who leads the efforts. *You* are the conductor of these changes. Realize the potential of your initiatives, and revel in the idea that you were part of brilliant academic "music" filling your halls with the resounding notes of learning and change.

Questions for Consideration and Discussion

1. How do you respond to the idea of "orchestration?" Why?

2. When do you notice an imbalance between the artistry of change and the masterminding of change?

3. How do you try to achieve a balance between the press for change and the support for the people doing the work?

What Are the Fundamental Ideas We Need to Be Thinking About?

Remember the scenario from Chapter One? Shirley Russell was focused on results as she attempted to lead teachers to implement more differentiated instructional strategies. She trusted her faculty to begin trying out the strategies. Principal Russell spent a considerable amount of time in classrooms looking for the changes and engaging in conversations with individuals, pressing them to begin trying out the new ideas. Anyone could have seen that Ms. Russell was busy in her support of differentiation. In spite of these efforts, she did not witness success, and nothing really improved at the school. Some of the reasons may be in her approach to the change and how she balanced the factors that could have better orchestrated lasting improvements at Culver Elementary School. These factors, or fundamental ideas, are central to transforming our leadership.

Let's begin with reflective questions that examine the way we are presently doing things. These reflections include questions such as:

- How am I going about my daily business now?

- How am I attending to the most pressing initiatives in my school?

- What is the nature of my interactions with teachers regarding my most important initiatives? Why is this the case?

- What is my approach to day-to-day dilemmas?

These reflective questions uncover the way we prefer to work with initiatives and people. Frequently, our approach as leaders tends to fall along the continuum of leader behavioral preferences shown in Figure 2.1.

Figure 2.1 The Maestro's Preferences Continuum

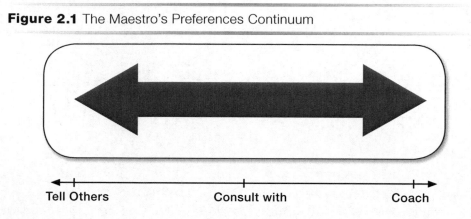

Tell Others   Consult with   Coach

Consider your day-to-day approach to work and the people with whom you work. Too often, many of us try to lead by "telling," essentially commanding others to follow our prescriptives. This preferred manner of getting things done causes us to be engulfed in daily tasks, many of them incredibly small and inconsequential. As a result, we are exhausted from working as hard as we possibly can and are astounded by the lack of results or at best, inconsistent results.

Some of us prefer a consultative style. We enjoy working with others and sharing our expertise, hoping to influence others into making more efficient and effective decisions about instruction. In essence, our job, as consulting leaders, is to convince others that our ideas are the best for them.

The problem with both telling and consulting methods is that they assume that the people with whom we are working are not as professional or knowledgeable as we are. When our job is to pull them toward better ideas, oftentimes our ideas for change are met with resistance.

Contrast these two methods with the coaching method. Leaders in the coaching world approach change as equals with the great majority of teachers and staff. The goal is for leaders to position ideas and actions, so they spark thinking among colleagues and decision-making about improvement. Coaching is not necessarily "soft." Indeed, some of the most powerful coaching strategies hold the other parties much more accountable than the "telling" or "consulting" methods of leadership. Think about it. When you tell someone to get on board with a change, you may be exerting authority, but you are also doing most of the heavy lifting. Instead of holding the other person accountable for thinking and learning, you are only holding the person accountable for following your order, however nicely put or sincerely felt.

Central to the idea of coaching others are two fundamental ideas. They are exemplified in Figure 2.2.

Figure 2.2 Relationships Plus Results Formula

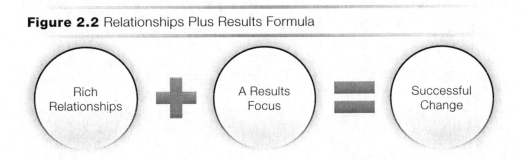

This formula creates the foundation for our work. Deceptively simple, this formula provides the foundation for the effective school leader as he or she thinks about how to orchestrate the necessary school changes. What is required is what Deal and Peterson (2000) first called "bifocal vision." The premise of a bifocal vision is that orchestrating change requires not only visionary thinking and management skill, but just as importantly, it requires ongoing professional relationships with others in the school to support the long-term motivation and commitment to the work. School change is exceedingly complex and requires these relationships to sustain it and to build a culture of "organizational citizenship" (Lewin and Regine 2000). This organizational citizenship promotes the feeling that we not only get a sense of accomplishment from successes in the work but also from the relationships that professionally feed us every day. What leaders will glean from this book, then, is this premium on the dual vision of leaders—building relationships while focusing on results and holding all accountable for the change. These ideas beg the question of all of us: *Are your daily actions both building relationships and focusing people on results?*

The leadership preferences continuum and the relationship plus results formula really demand that the effective maestro incorporate both as he or she makes individual decisions about how to work with each teacher at the school campus. In effect, these ideas are encouraging, and yet they demand that the maestro adopt a differentiated approach to working with the adults in the school. The complexity of knowing how to work with individual teachers may seem overwhelming, unless the maestro has a set of key concepts to construct a framework—a schema of sorts—for orchestrating the kinds of actions that will lead to sustained improvement. These key concepts, shown in Figure 2.3, form the foundation for this book and the key elements for the leader to consider as he or she develops differentiated strategies for working with the adults in the school.

Figure 2.3 Orchestration: The School Leader's Framework

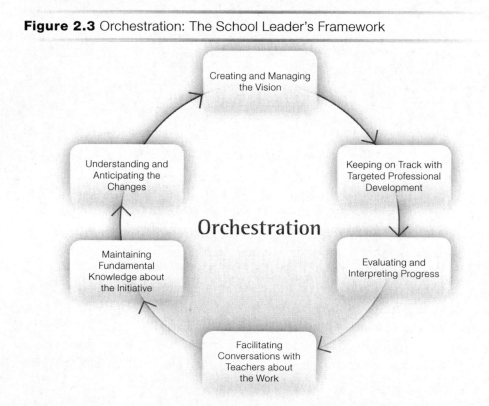

The maestro, then, must consider these six elements simultaneously in thinking about leading the changes at his or her school. In addition, the leader must consider these elements in thinking about how each of his or her teachers is responding to the need for change, and adopt a differentiated approach to working with each individual or groups of individuals (Kise 2006). In other words, people really react in a personal way to the demand for change; just as in working with students, there is no one approach or pathway that works for all. It is important to remember that the vast majority of teachers want to do well at their school. Therefore, the differentiated approach to working with teachers may provide a more tailored and effective way of addressing how individuals are reacting to the changes. This allows the leader to better match actions with individual personalities to encourage teachers to make the next step toward institutionalizing the needed improvements, so they can continue to feel successful in contributing to a universally important cause—educating our students more effectively.

It is hard to coach others—building relationships while focusing on results—unless each of us as leaders operates from a schema that arrives at positive beliefs about teachers and staff and how successful they want to be. In keeping with this reflective chapter, our next task is to ruthlessly examine our fundamental beliefs about the people with whom we work. The vast majority of teachers and school staff members are working as hard as they feel they can, and they want to experience success every day. While this basic premise may sound good to all of us (and we would never admit that we don't believe it), it is important at this point to examine these core beliefs. Consider the following and reflect on whether or not you strongly agree with each of the following beliefs.

If we fundamentally agree with each of these beliefs, it is next to impossible to approach orchestration of change from a "telling" point of view since that preferred set of behaviors undermines the kinds of relationships and daily actions mandated by these beliefs. In effect, these beliefs demand a more personalized approach with people, focusing on simultaneous relationship-building while holding all staff members accountable for continuous growth and improvement.

Finish your reflection on these big ideas by putting yourself to the test. For one or two days, make some notes about your own work in orchestrating change at your school or schools. You may want to reproduce Figure 2.4 electronically and complete it over several days. Then, take stock of where you square with these beliefs about a) telling, b) consulting, c) coaching, and d) your beliefs about teachers.

Figure 2.4 My Orchestration Log

Contact	Nature of the Conversation or Action	Telling?	Some Telling?	Consulting?	Consulting and a Little Coaching?	Coaching?

For each critical action throughout the this process of reflection, log the primary contact and the nature of the action or conversation. Then, put yourself to the reflective test. If your overall behavior and tone was to tell the person what to do or accomplish, put an *X* in the telling column for that contact and action. Continue to log all of your major conversations and actions for the two days and put an *X* marking the best fit for your behavior and tone. Then, after two days of logging these actions and conversations, look at the patterns. What do you see? What does that say about your preferences and how you work with people? Do your actions and words project beliefs that you regret?

Thinking About the Nature of Your Interventions

This log, if completed, documents the variety of interventions the school leader has with other individuals in the school. We now know that effective school leadership often requires the maestro to intervene to increase the potential for the initiative to become more effective and long-lasting. Hall and Hord (2010, 105) describe the idea of intervention to be "any action or event that influences the individuals involved or expected to be involved in the process." Therefore, in thinking about our framework for orchestrating change, the assumption is that leaders will first consider the six elements:

- Creating and managing the vision

- Keeping on track with targeted professional development

- Evaluating and interpreting progress

- Facilitating conversations with teachers about the work

- Maintaining fundamental knowledge about the initiative

- Understanding and anticipating the next changes

The leader will then consider "where his or her teachers are" in relation to the anticipated changes and provide differentiated interventions. Such interventions may include actions such as sending a new article supporting the initiative to selected teachers, discussing progress and next steps with a teacher, and personally gathering additional information about the nature of the initiative for personal development. What is important to remember is that the maestro is considering actions he or she must take in direct relationship to the initiative. In other words, the maestro does not set up conditions for the initiative to be successful and then sit on the sidelines and watch it unfold. We know that successful implementation requires daily attention to the initiative, deliberate actions on the leader's part to move it forward and to keep progress steady toward institutionalization.

Interestingly, events are circumstances that happen outside the deliberation and intention of the maestro (Hall and Hord 2010, 106). The leader must also notice and consider these events that were not planned, yet influence the progress of the initiative. Examples of events include the following:

- Conflicts that erupt among teachers about the initiative that derail the momentum of planning

- A conversation that results, accidentally, in misconceptions about the initiative

- An opportunity for teachers to struggle with an implementation dilemma

- Unexpected positive results and immediate relationships with an outside consultant supporting the initiative

Events can have positive or hindering consequences in relation to the initiative. What is important is that the leader is aware of them and decides whether or not to intervene.

There is, then, a critical relationship of the initiative to the maestro. This relationship demands a consistent and regular review of the six critical elements of orchestration and calibrating possible interventions to the individual or individuals for targeted relationship building and results-focused success. This describes the essence of the philosophy of change that permeates this book. Consider these reflective questions as you dive into each element of the maestro's collection of critical concepts:

Questions for Consideration and Discussion

1. What is your preferred style of working with people? Does it work? When does it backfire and why?

2. How do you react to the idea that rich relationships plus a results focus equals successful change? Does this formula match with your actions? Why or why not?

3. Do you believe all interventions are created equal? Can you examine your interventions in the last week? How successful were they? How do you know?

4. Identify an example of an event that you would allow to happen in order to advance the initiative. Why is that important?

5. Why is it important for leaders to examine their philosophies about people and change before orchestrating and masterminding an initiative?

What Will Make My Actions Effective?

Culver Elementary School principal, Shirley Russell, had done her homework. After collecting the data to support the changes she tried to orchestrate, she led her team through a book study in which they examined the fundamentals of differentiated instruction. She scheduled the professional development and attended every session. So why did the initiative fall flat during the first year of implementation? Let's examine what Ms. Russell needed to consider as she initiated the work. At the end of this chapter, reflect again on Principal Russell's work and dilemmas. How would you have done it differently based on the ideas in this chapter?

The change that school leaders need only happens through a carefully orchestrated series of steps and supports through the initiative's life span. Compounding the work is the simple fact that school maestros may not be able to deeply know or understand the complexities of each of the instructional improvements they are expected to lead.

However, it is important to understand that maestros need not know each of their initiatives in the same way that they would expect their teachers to know and understand the initiatives. To put it another way, school leaders work to ensure that their teachers have the time and resources to deeply understand the instructional initiative in terms of implementation—how it looks in the classroom, how to deepen the work for more profound student results, and how to assess on a daily basis to see if those results are being attained and are leading students toward the attainment of the major concepts of the initiative—the essential driving ideas that teachers hope students will remember long after their involvement in the instruction.

School leaders, however, need to know and understand the instructional initiative "big ideas" in a related but unique way. Leaders must keep the overall goals of the initiative, the "big ideas," in mind on a daily basis, so that as they are in classrooms and talking with teachers, they are aware if the results they are seeing and hearing are getting the school closer to the attainment of the overall goals of the initiative. Perhaps Shirley Russell did not keep the fundamentals—the big ideas of the initiative—in mind as she was so busy telling people to implement the practices and assuming that because everything seemed so positive that she must be experiencing success.

Therefore, while both groups, teachers and school leaders, must know the big ideas behind the instructional initiative, they are using different forms of assessment to see if the big ideas are being achieved. Teachers are using student performance information and informal assessment to ascertain the accomplishment of the big ideas, while school leaders are looking at conversations, classroom observations, and other forms of evidence to determine how close or how far away they are from the initiative's overall reason for being. This chapter addresses the actions the leaders must take to see if the work of the initiative is progressing and if the big ideas of the work are being actualized.

> **Concepts and Skills in This Chapter:**
>
> - The "backward" way to think about the initiative
> - The difference between the "what" and the "how" of orchestration
> - Choices in how to support the initiative
> - Applying "heat" and "light" to make things happen

Choosing a Backward Way to Think about and Act on the Initiative

Although it appears somewhat antithetical to school leaders' thinking, a backward design for orchestrating a school initiative is preferred. Yet, as Wiggins and McTighe remind us (2007), "although backward design makes sense for [the leader's] planning, its logic is not always followed within the hectic operation of schools and districts" (205). The authors remind us that the failure to adhere to the concepts behind a backward design to their work may lead to inevitable variations on the "twin sins" of reform planning (2007). Those sins are detailed in Figure 3.1.

Figure 3.1 The "Twin Sins" of School Reform

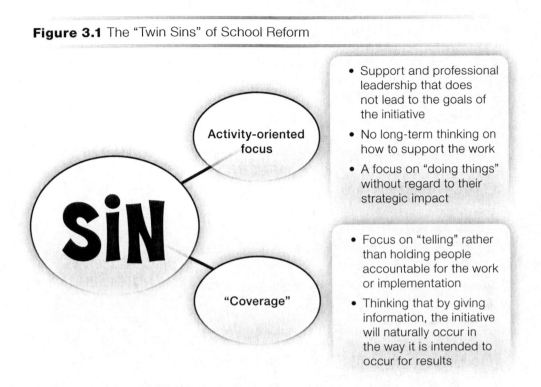

So what is backward planning, and why is this preferable to school leaders? In essence, backward planning is thinking like a maestro—knowing the vision for the performance of the school first and letting that vision drive the carefully-managed work. Wiggins and McTighe (2007) translate backward planning in another way. They liken it to the work in architecture. In building something, the vision of the overall design is needed but insufficient. Detailed strategic blueprints must be produced and followed for turning the vision into strategic, coordinated action. Instead of jumping into arbitrary, activity-focused moves that may make us feel like something is being accomplished, they advocate the backward planning design for strategic, coherent, understandable, and sustainable reform. Based on Wiggins's and McTighe's work, the successful school maestro orchestrates change through the expanded backward planning design shown in Figure 3.2.

Figure 3.2 Orchestrating through the Backward Design

1
- What is your overall vision for this initiative?
- What will our school look like when we have fully achieved this?
- What do teachers and staff need to know and be able to do in order for us to achieve this year's goals for this initiative?

2
- How will we know that we are experiencing success?
- What are the key indicators, and where will we get that evidence?
- How will we be able to interpret that evidence to lead us to course corrections?

3
- What is our plan for this year?
- What will be leadership's major actions?
- What resources are needed?
- Is our evaluation timeline built into our actions?

This approach to the maestro's work prevents him or her from committing the two sins of planning—being activity focused and merely assuming that by talking about the work and giving information, the initative will proceed. By holding the vision firmly and being able to articulate the vision into yearly plans, the maestro is forced to consider the goal first and the evidence second before he or she can commit to a plan. The backward planning design breaks the predictable dilemma that most school leaders find themselves in—feeling that they have been working hard but are achieving little.

What Should We Know about the Initiative?

The school maestro must be familiar enough with the initiative to understand the essential ideas behind the initiative. These enduring ideas include what is central or core to the initiative. His or her conversations with teachers, then, must focus on these enduring essential ideas behind the initiative, so there is coherent and consistent work to drive the implementation of the initiative toward the enduring principles behind it, and the school leader is gathering evidence related to the intended results of his or her actions.

Knowing the essential ideas undergirding an initiative is similar to the work that school leaders assume when supporting the implementation of new rigorous curriculum and learning standards. In understanding new standards, it is "essential" to understand the major shifts intended by the standards implementation. These shifts can include redirection away from the "inch-deep, mile-wide" curriculum that is in most mathematics programs, a coherent balance of concepts and skills and students working on projects or mathematical tasks over time. The school leader may not know discrete standards for subjects or teaching practices related to "important knowledge" students must have in the subject, but he or she can, if knowledgeable of the big enduring understandings in mathematics, discuss these essential concepts with teachers without having discrete knowledge of how to teach each concept. Armed with this knowledge of the new standards, the school maestro can engage teachers in conversations with questions such as these:

- What was the purpose of the lesson today?

- How did the lesson build endurance and "grit" with the students?

- How did this lesson relate to the big shifts in instruction we are seeking?

- How did you know the teaching segment was successful, and how does that lead to your next progression of teaching and skills?

This constitutes the "what" of the school maestro's work—to be supremely knowledgeable of the essential elements of the initiative, so his or her work, conversations, and evidence are focused on these elements. Moreover, these enduring, essential elements of the initiative must be reflected in the vision for the initiative. (See Chapter Four for more on creating the vision for the initiative.)

How Can We Support Change and the Initiative?

When the school maestro has the knowledge of "what" the initiative is intended to achieve, he or she must then consider actions which will help accelerate and sustain movement toward these goals. Any action or event which influences the individuals involved in the change toward the initiative is considered an intervention (Hall and Hord 2010). Sometimes, circumstances and events can alter the direction and progress of the initiative. In many cases, these circumstances and events happen outside deliberations, and plans for the change can be monitored by the school maestro in terms of subsequent action on his or her part. Most often, however, the initiative will not flourish unless it is supported by specific actions by the maestro—deliberate, focused "moves" on the leader's part.

There are six specific actions which fall under the maestro's deliberate strategies to sustain the initiative. The actions address what the evidence points out as the "need" at that specific moment in the initiative's life span. Figure 3.3 illustrates how these actions and "needs" connect.

Figure 3.3 Six Functions of Need-Related Interventions

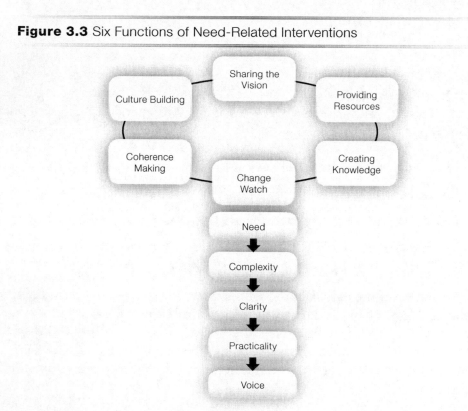

A Backward Explanation of the Graphic

In keeping with the backward planning design, an explanation of the five needs identified in Figure 3.3 is needed first (Fullan 2007):

Need: Do teachers, in understanding the overarching purpose of the initiative, feel that this initiative is the right one for this time in their lives? Do they feel that the initiative fulfills a need for either them or their students? In some cases, the school maestro may feel that the initiative is sorely needed, but because of a lack of data shared with the staff, the teachers may not experience the same urgency.

Complexity: In some cases, teachers may experience the need, but because of the complexity of the initiative, not be compelled to action. Some initiatives, because they are systemic, may appear to be overwhelming to the teachers.

Clarity: Once again, is a lack of specific and cogent communication the problem? If so, clarity may be the need. Fullan (2007) reminds us that teachers may be able to talk about the proposed change and the initiative and may believe that they "understand" the initiative and the work behind it, but just because they can talk about it, doesn't mean they comprehend the steps for implementation, or the intended results or enduring ideas behind the initiative.

Practicality: Related to "need," practicality speaks to the practical application of the initiative. Do teachers understand the practical benefits, either to themselves or to their students? Does the initiative fit with the other demands in their day and reinforce other instructional practices they are being held responsible for? Are they experiencing short-term wins that reinforce the practical nature and the benefits of the initiative?

Voice: Are teachers involved in helping to troubleshoot the initiative? Do teachers feel that their voices were heard when the initiative was selected? Are the opinions of teachers solicited and heard during all parts of the initiative's life span?

When the need has been identified, then the maestro is free to consider the six actions that represent the "job description" of the leader. These six actions are influenced by the work of Hall and Hord (2010).

Sharing the Vision: Often, if there is a perceived lack of need for the initiative or if there is confusion as to the intent of the initiative, the maestro will find that he or she needs to communicate the vision in understandable words and concepts. This helps teachers forge their own mental images of the change effort and what it will look like when each of the yearly visions is actualized. Indeed, change leaders find that they must continuously communicate this vision to enable the implementers to move toward deep implementation of the changes.

Providing Resources: Resources are necessary to help move the vision toward operation. The leader's consideration of resources includes time, materials, and policies; and all supportive elements that are seen to be necessary to encourage teachers to take the initiative and begin putting it into action in their classrooms. The lack of resources, or the front loading of resources that dwindle when teachers are in the throes of implementation, will sabotage even the most carefully planned change initiative. The maestro must plan resource allocation and distribution as carefully as he or she has planned the overall initiative—allowing the resources to change and adjust over time.

Creating Knowledge: Professional development often propels the beginning of major initiatives. Unfortunately, most professional development is, once again, front loaded. The fact of the matter is that professional development is needed at all stages of the initiative's life span. The needs and interests of the teacher implementers change over time as they get more comfortable with the change and move its implementation to deeper levels. Thus, the change leader will want to carefully plan professional development as their teachers move from novice implementation to expert. In addition, maestros must remember that training is effective for the initiation of the change, but woefully inadequate as teachers move into actual implementation. (See Chapter 6 for more about professional development and how to incorporate it into plans.)

Change Watch: Another way to describe "change watch" is checking on progress along the way. Maestros understand that the progress of the change needs to be evaluated on a regular basis. If complexity seems to be a need, the leader will want to break the change into smaller, more short-term changes. This will help teachers understand that the complexity is actually a series of well-planned, more easily attainable changes on their part. So, "change watch" is really two concepts for the maestro—watching the changes over time and getting a sense of the changes through his or her formative assessment and communicating the change in small moves for the teachers. The yearly vision for the initiative will help support both of these management concepts for the maestro.

Coherence Making: For the maestro, coherence making is an incredibly important action. If practicality seems to be an issue, it may be that teachers do not see how this initiative is connected to other efforts on their part. These other efforts could include other initiatives or goals for the school, district, or country. People seek coherence in their actions and are gratified when they understand that multiple initiatives are indeed connected in terms of their big ideas. Seeking coherence enables implementers to stay the course in that their efforts are seen as contributing to the larger picture of connected initiatives. In addition, coherence making means that the leader continually finds information and data and shares it with teacher implementers to help them see the fruits of their substantial labor.

Culture Building: The maestro cannot neglect the culture or climate of the school to support the changes prescribed by the initiative. In fact, when "voice" may be an issue, it can be that the culture of the school is not developed in a way to promote problem solving, conversation, and the contextual elements that support successful implementation. As written in Hall and Hord (2010), it is recommended that the leader take actions to create a context of experimentation, support, conversation, and risk taking by considering these actions:

- Shape the physical features of the building context by manipulating schedules and structures such as faculty meetings, so people can have the time to share improvement ideas.

- Model the behaviors and norms desired by the staff by interacting and cooperating with all staff and being highly visible to teachers when implementation is desired.

- Teach and coach by sharing materials and being highly aware of the initiative.

- Address conflict by dealing with the difficulties and building unified collaboration.

- Address any building, policy, or material needs carefully.

Applying "Heat" and "Light" to Make Things Happen

As stated in the introduction, successful maneuvering of multiple initiatives requires the skill of orchestrating. This is not only the artistic part of the work—the leadership, if you will—but it also includes the collection of resources, planning, and careful management. Just as the concert maestro skillfully and artistically joins multiple voices and sounds into a beautiful piece of music, the school leader orchestrates, through vision, motivation, conversation, management, and the development of human potential, the "skilled will" to make the changes happen. Robert Quinn describes leadership in this way:

"We concluded that CEOs are expected to play four general competing roles: vision setter, motivator, analyzer, and taskmaster. Based on these domains, the model suggests four demands that all top managers must attend: the need for people, for innovation, for efficiency, and for performance."

—Robert Quinn (1996, 148)

These demands led Quinn to suggest two broad roles that are often viewed as competing. These two roles are defined in terms of transactional and transformational roles in Figure 3.4.

Figure 3.4 Transactional and Transformational Roles

Transactional Role (Heat)	Transformational Role (Light)
• The demand for efficiency and getting the work done based on information and data • A focus on the operating systems of the school	• The need for people in the organization to be motivated around the work • A focus on the organization and the culture of the organization to support the change
• A constant demand for performance and sustained change and improvement • A focus on the market and what the expectations are for improvement	• The demand for experimentation and innovation • A focus on the future of the school and its ability to keep up with the most important and needed changes

(Adapted from Quinn 1996)

Carol Tomlinson, well-known educator and author, has often referred to transactional as the "heat" and transformational as the "light" in school leadership. Indeed, the "heat" role is all about getting the work done and efficiency in improvement. The "light" role is about creating systems to support it, relationships, understanding the vision or moral purpose for the work, and supporting change through experimentation.

In his work, Quinn (1996) found that most business CEOs frequently engaged in transactional behaviors—applying the "heat" to get the work done. The question that Quinn posed was whether or not CEOs who performed both roles get different results from those who emphasize only the transactional aspects of their work. Their answer was yes, and they found significant information that told his researchers that the highest levels of performance were achieved by CEOs who frequently engage in both roles on a consistent and related basis.

In thinking about orchestrating, then, it seems that success for the leader lies in the integration and seamless performance of both kinds of roles, reinforcing people, demanding experimentation toward the vision, maximizing efficiency, and holding people accountable for performance. Successful implementation of any initiative rests its hope on remembering what is good for the organization, but at the same time, understanding the real role in getting things done. The ideas in the chapters to follow detail specifics that reinforce the six kinds of interventions described in the previous pages. Finally, the school maestro has the tools and the ideas in one place to help him or her create the lasting concert of improvement that is so desperately needed!

Orchestrating Big Ideas:

- Think first about the vision and goals for the initiative before you contemplate your actions to support it. Let the goals drive your choice of actions.

- Match the need presented in the initiative with a choice among six functions of actions on your part.

- The application of both heat (masterminding) and light (orchestration) is necessary for effective, long-lasting implementation of the initiative.

Questions for Consideration and Discussion

1. Can you think of a previous initiative when you focused on your actions without paying attention first to the vision? What happened and why? How would you lead that initiative differently now?

2. What are the kinds of needs that present themselves at your school? How do they compare with the needs described in this chapter?

3. Do you lean toward more "heat" than "light?" Why do you find yourself leaning towards it? How is this chapter helping you think differently about the combination of heat and light? Why?

How Do I Develop a Vision for This Initiative?

School leaders will not be successful in orchestrating the implementation of an initiative unless the people associated with the initiative can accurately describe what the change should look like. Having a vision of the change—a clear, operational description of the desired changes—is therefore critical to a leader's work. The school maestro must effectively and efficiently craft this overall vision for the initiative and then use it as a "coalescing point" for communication and motivation for participating staff to not only achieve the vision but collaborate with the school leaders in charting the progress. The vision essentially addresses the question, "If we don't know what success looks like, how can we know if we got there?"

Vision statements are often confused with mission statements; this confusion, combined with the idea that many visions and missions are often crafted in vague and paralyzing language, contributes to the bad rap that visions often have with school leaders and teachers. Figure 4.1 illustrates the fundamental differences between vision (the "what") and mission (the "how").

Figure 4.1 Understanding Differences Between Vision and Mission Statements

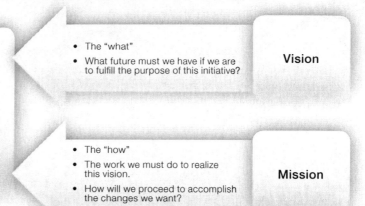

Mission and vision are often used interchangeably. When applying the terms to school change, they represent different concepts.

- The "what"
- What future must we have if we are to fulfill the purpose of this initiative?

Vision

- The "how"
- The work we must do to realize this vision.
- How will we proceed to accomplish the changes we want?

Mission

This chapter takes a somewhat nontraditional approach to the vision. This nontraditional approach asks the school leaders to draft a vision for the initiative, not the school as a whole. This vision is the description of what school looks like after the successful implementation of the initiative. The creation of an initiative vision encourages the participants to focus on the implementation of the most important work at the school rather than adhere to more vague, general expectations of what school is to be. In addition, many vision-producing processes are long and intensive. The bias here is to spend the valuable collaborative energy to quickly create a vision for guidance of progress toward the anticipated change. Unlike laborious vision- or mission-creation processes, the processes outlined here are to be accomplished in a matter of hours rather than days. Creating the initiative's vision propels the work into implementation faster. The vision accelerates the work by functioning to periodically evaluate the work, rather than serving as a useless piece sitting on a shelf, untouched and unused to manage the work or focus the communication about the work.

The vision detailed in this chapter must serve two simultaneous purposes—the maestro of change must not only facilitate an overall vision for the initiative that is understandable and galvanizing to school leaders and teachers, but he or she must also be able to break the vision down into manageable, obtainable operational visions for each year of work in that initiative. These operational, one-year visions for the initiative are crucial for orchestrating the change. When people leading and implementing the initiative have a clear picture of the changes desired just for this year, they can more easily "see themselves in the change" and will be willing to work toward this yearly set of initiative goals.

Concepts and Skills in This Chapter:

- Definition of an effective vision statement
- Designing the overall vision for the initiative
- Using the vision to orchestrate from initiation to effective implementation
- Designing the overall vision for the initiative
- Creating the yearly operational visions through vision "horizoning"
- Creating "short term wins" to sustain motivation and energy

The Vision Statement Defined

One of the most easily understood definitions of a vision is "a realistic, credible, attractive future for the organization" (DuFour, DuFour, and Eaker 2008, 472). The vision essentially attempts to describe the change we are trying to create by successfully implementing the initiative. The vision statement is the "what" of the work. It lends guidance to how to accomplish the work of the initiative, but it stops short of detailing the actions leaders must orchestrate to make the initiative successful. To put it another way, the vision, like the maestro's work, details the change he or she wants participants to feel, notice, and actualize regarding the school's initiative. Use the following checklist to determine the effective vision for your initiative (DuFour, DuFour, and Eaker 2008):

Does the Vision for Your Initiative:

- Help convey a picture of what the change will look like?

- Appeal to the long-term interests of the people who work there?

- Seem realistic?

- Seem focused and clear enough to provide guidance in decision making?

- Appear flexible enough to allow for individual responses in light of changing conditions in the school?

- Allow for communication and easy explanation?

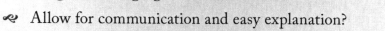

The initiative's vision must be useful to not only the leader of change but also the participants of the anticipated change. Indeed, the vision must "galvanize (attract) the deep energies and commitment of organization members to make desirable things happen" (Fullan 2001, 115). The vision can influence this coalescence of energies and actions only when it is shared at all levels of the organization and is further enhanced by the experiences people have as they are working toward the vision for the initiative. Simply put, living the vision, if clearly understood by all participants, enhances their understanding of what the initiative is trying to achieve and adds to the common vocabulary of the participants as they talk about the change. Peter Senge (1999) refers to this close and necessary association with the vision as "seeing our [future] environment as directly and close as we are able" (530). In truth, the vision, if it is to galvanize people around ideas and push them to live the vision in their own realm, must work to focus efforts rather than fragment them. If this focus is to occur, the participants in the change must then craft the vision collaboratively if it is to attract and sustain the focus and energies of participants.

The simple creation of a vision for the initiative is only part of the challenge for the change maestro. The school leader must orchestrate any school initiative with a combination of artistic strategies to keep the vision for the change alive with the participants well into the implementation of the change. This maestro cannot adequately orchestrate the initiative without first understanding the way any initiative tends to "live" in a school over time. Insights as to the change life span will help the effective leader realize when the vision needs to re-emerge to pull people together and mobilize their efforts.

Most educators see three distinct, developmental phases to the change process (Fullan 2007), summarized in Figure 4.2.

Figure 4.2 The Life Span of a School Initiative

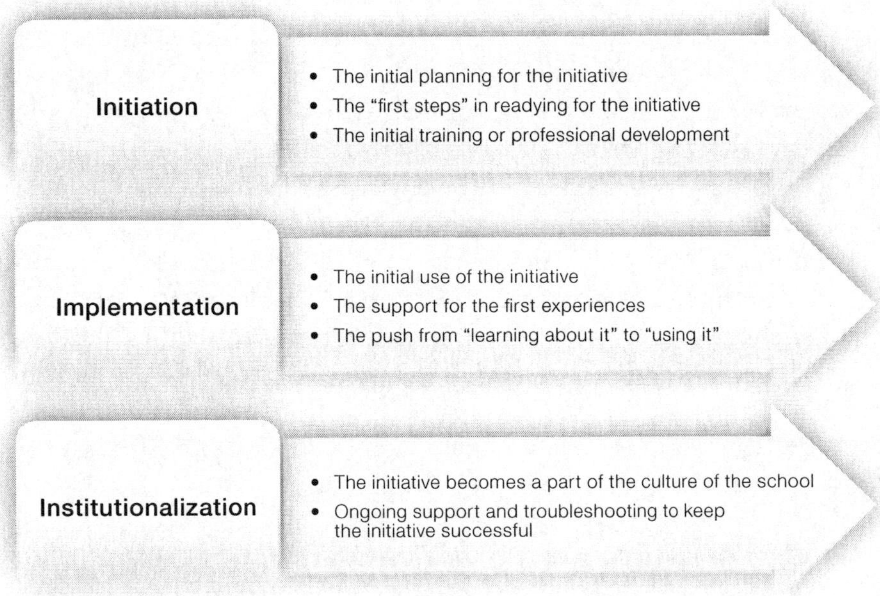

Initiation
- The initial planning for the initiative
- The "first steps" in readying for the initiative
- The initial training or professional development

Implementation
- The initial use of the initiative
- The support for the first experiences
- The push from "learning about it" to "using it"

Institutionalization
- The initiative becomes a part of the culture of the school
- Ongoing support and troubleshooting to keep the initiative successful

Initiation

Initiation is the work, planning, and initial steps in making the change operational. The impetus for the change may come from a variety of sources. In schools where rapid-fire change is a way of life, it is probably more relevant to look at effective strategies to get an initiative started instead of discussing the various sources for the change.

On a positive note, people are often very excited at the beginning of an initiative. During this initiation phase, champions frequently campaign for the initiative and point out its alleged benefits. One of the dilemmas for the school leader is how to effectively get the critical mass of participants receptive to the initiative and hopeful for its prospects to make positive change. Fullan (2007) points out that in schools, there can still be a great deal of inertia, requiring great energy to overcome. This dilemma is where a thoughtful process to define the change, using the vision, is instrumental to the change leader.

Thus, it is important that an overall vision for the initiative is created during the first part of the initiative—the "beginning and planning" phase. More information on the process for creating the vision is found later in this chapter. Through the creation of energy and the collaborative process of creating "what we want the initiative to achieve," the vision is very beneficial at the initiation phase of the change to coalesce excitement about the change and form a common vocabulary, a way of talking about the proposed change in terms of the unique qualities of the initiative. During the last part of the initiation phase, a "first-year" vision or statement of what the change should look like at the end of the first year of implementation should be crafted as well. This first-year vision will serve to guide the first real steps toward implementation. More information about the details for crafting the first-year vision is included later in this chapter. If the vision is to be effective at this phase, follow these tips:

Orchestrating the Vision during the Initiation Phase:

- Create the long-range vision for the initiation (early on) and the first-year operational vision (right before implementation) during this change phase.

- Use key words in the vision to stress mobilization and the "moral purpose" of the change (Fullan 2001).

- Use the long-range overall vision to tie into other initiatives the staff are involved in to see the alignment and help them understand the "big picture."

Implementation

If initiation is the beginning planning stage and readying the school for the initiative, then implementation is "where the rubber meets the road." Implementation "involves the first experiences in attempting to put a reform or idea into practice" (Fullan 2007, 65). While there is often great energy around the first use of the initiative, the leader must remember that actual implementation takes much more than one year—often complete implementation takes anywhere from three to five years of effort. The issues that arise in the second or third year of implementation will be much different from the issues that arise during the first year of implementation. The effective maestro of change realizes that a dangerous period during implementation is the implementation "dip," where the implementation of the initiative often meets management challenges and participants may lose enthusiasm for the change or even attempt to abandon the change. You will remember our Culver Elementary School example as a classic illustration of the implementation dip. Although this dip occurred relatively quickly at Culver, it certainly was indicative of the dangers of implementation. Teachers began to complain about the changes, had difficulty implementing them beyond superficial strategies, and began lobbying openly to discard the change. In essence, the teachers at Culver Elementary tried really hard to abandon the practices because they had trouble managing them.

During implementation, the school leader must make use of each year's operational vision to keep momentum constant and to keep the initiative first and foremost in participants' minds and actions. Because of this need, it will be necessary for the leader and staff to craft the next year's vision using the same process outlined later in this chapter. Each new one-year operational vision serves as the rallying cry for the change, defining in clear, practical language the change that is expected for this year. Again, Shirley Russell, at Culver Elementary School, wrongly assumed that all teachers carried a mental vision of what the changes at Culver would look like. Her lack of a written, vibrant vision was one of the factors contributing to the demise of the initiative because teachers really did not know what they were exactly "shooting for."

There are key factors that affect the implementation of the initiative that relate directly to the nature of the change itself (Fullan 2007). These factors and clarifying questions are need, clarity, complexity, quality, and practicality.

Key Factors Affecting the Implementation Phase:

- **Need:** How are our needs being met by the initiative, and are we making some progress using it?

- **Clarity:** Do we have a clear picture of what we are supposed to be doing differently?

- **Complexity:** How difficult and extensive is the change being sought?

- **Quality and Practicality:** How important is the initiative, and how useful is it to me?

The effective change leader understands the critical role the vision plays in continuing implementation of the initiative for several years. First, to effectively orchestrate implementation, the yearly vision should be used to focus the efforts of the participants and to remind them of the short-term successes they are having based on that yearly vision. In addition, the vision should be used to continue to get clarity of what is being attempted. The yearly vision, if in operational terms, will provide that sense of "what are we trying to achieve this year?"

Perhaps the most critical point to remember is that when the going gets tough and participants are having dilemmas implementing the initiative, leaders can use the yearly vision to remind them what their goals really are. This reminder is critical, as many teachers assume that the school leaders expect massive, quick changes to their classroom instruction. Using the yearly vision breaks this perception of massive changes down into smaller, more manageable, more "doable" steps or components. In summary, use the following tips during implentation:

Orchestrating the Vision during the Implementation Phase:

- Create the shorter, more operational yearly visions to guide the work and focus the conversations with the participants.

- Use the yearly vision to evaluate the progress being seen in classroom implementation.

- Focus frustrated practitioners by reminding them of your yearly vision for the initiative and what success looks like.

- Use the operational, yearly vision to break the complexity of the initiative down into more manageable parts or components.

- Use the operational, yearly vision to highlight celebrations for participants.

- Post the yearly vision in a common workroom for all to see.

Institutionalization

Institutionalization signals the fact that the initiative has been incorporated tight into the mainstream of the school. During the institutionalization phase of the change, participants simply don't talk about the initiative much anymore. The change, in fact, has become a part of the fabric of "the way we do things around here." While this phase seems to signal a natural and desired ending to the efforts to move an initiative, nothing could be further from the truth. In fact, during the institutionalization phase, the effective change maestro uses that year's operational vision to move the participants even closer to the desired, overall vision for the initiative.

A dilemma to institutionalization is that often this phase signals a reduction of funding for the initiative. During this phase, the initiative begins to lose its moniker of a "special project" and, much to the leader's dismay, this reduction of special change status may also signal a lack of interest or continued effort by participants. During this phase, then, the change leader must ensure that the initiative becomes reflected in how the school is structured, through policy and regulations.

Another challenge to institutionalization is staff turnover. The effective change leader uses that year's operational vision to point out to new participants what the change is all about and demands support for the initiative through the effective continual communication of that year's operational vision.

When the leader senses institutionalization of the initiative, he or she uses the vision to accomplish the following:

Orchestrating the Vision During the Institutionalization Phase:

- The yearly operational visions will be closer to the overall vision for the initiative. Use the year's operational vision to point out how close participants are getting to the overall institutionalization of the initiative.

- Focus the efforts of new staff members by communicating the year's operational vision to them and asking for their efforts to implement the initiative in their classrooms.

- Plan for how the initiative can become a part of standard operating procedures by creating regulations, structures, or policies to support institutionalization.

- Plan for institutionalization by discussing with participants the expectations for institutionalization and how this initiative must become a component of everyday practice.

Designing the Overall Vision for the Initiative

The purpose of creating an overall vision for the initiative is to create that initial driver for this work and provide the key vocabulary and foundation for dialogue that the change leader and participants will have throughout the process. This vision statement is the foundation from which yearly operational visions will be developed. Creating the initiative's overall vision should be as collaborative as possible. Widespread participation and dialogue will enhance the chance that the vision will speak to everyone involved and will forge understanding of the purpose of this major undertaking. Successful masterminding of a vision will involve these steps:

Vision Creation Leader Preparation:

- ❑ Complete professional development for awareness and information about the initiative.

- ❑ Gauge all participants' understanding of the initiative and working knowledge of the basics of it.

- ❑ Determine if all participating staff members have sufficient background knowledge in the content area (if necessary) to help create a vision statement for the initiative.

- ❑ Invite selected (or volunteer) participants to help you design a vision for the initiative and explain the rationale for the work.

- ❑ Create a setting where the participants can work comfortably and think critically.

- ❑ Plan for seating of 4–6 participants at small tables for conversation and small group work.

- ❑ Gather any key materials that will help explain the initiative.

- ❑ Collect all materials for the design work (see list below).

- ❑ Plan on three hours to create the vision.

Necessary Materials:

- ❑ chart paper and chart stand
- ❑ blank walls for posting of ideas
- ❑ index cards
- ❑ half sheets card stock (about 10 for each participant)
- ❑ markers
- ❑ tape for the walls
- ❑ colored sticker dots (about 8–10 per participant) (for consensus building)

Orchestrating the Vision–Building Process

The energy in this meeting should be optimistic. Open with introductory remarks and reinforce the value that each participant will bring to the endeavor. Remind them of the value that the vision will have for the initiative (see this chapter for those key ideas). After logistical details, invite the participants to dialogue about the initiative for a few minutes. This initial dialogue will allow the participants to begin imagining the benefits that the initiative will bring to the school. Then, use the following steps for the actual design of the initiative's vision.

Participants should be seated comfortably in groups of 4–6 people at small tables for conversation. First, engage them in imagining how the school will be different as a result of the initiative. Guide them into speculating how the school will be different for the key stakeholders of the initiative, such as students, teachers, or school leaders. Ask them to consider how the school will be different as a result of this initiative. Will structures change their schedules, procedures, or ways of operating? See Figure 4.3 for key groups of people and concepts involved in changing the school structure.

Figure 4.3 The Vision Question

When this initiative is fully in place, how do you think our school will be changed? Think about these key groups and our school structure.

Students

Teachers

Parents

Community

School

During this speculation, ask each participant to take an index card and write their ideas, thinking of how they expect each of the groups to be changed as a result of the unique attributes and goals of this initiative. Then, encourage them to also consider how they believe the school will be different as a result of the initiative. Give them several minutes to complete their individual "idea writing." Then, rearrange the participants by choice or assign tables according to the following groups: students, teachers, parents, community, and school. They should then determine which groups would be most affected by the initiative. It may be necessary to assign several tables or groups the same area.

Assign each table one of the agreed-upon stakeholder groups, such as students or teachers. Then, display the following question for all to see:

Think about your assigned group or aspect. If we implement this initiative well, how will your group be changed? What will be different?

Ask table participants to share their individual index card ideas only if their ideas pertain to their assigned group. During this sharing of ideas, ask the table participants to begin to write each powerful idea on one of the half sheets of card stock. Continue this process until all members have exhausted their personal lists and have one group list pertaining to their assignment.

Next, ask one representative from each table group to post all of the half sheets of card stock under appropriately titled large sheets of chart paper (see Figure 4.4). Create one chart paper sheet for students, one sheet for teachers, and so on. Place these sheets and the card stock ideas on one wall for group analysis and discussion.

Figure 4.4 Example of Vision Brainstorming

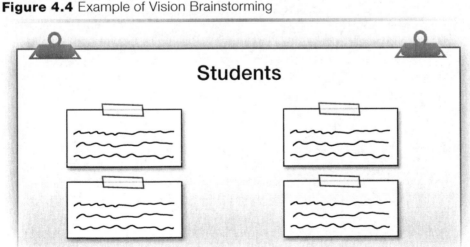

Facilitate a process where the group discusses and analyzes all of the ideas on the individual pieces of chart paper. If necessary, group similar ideas on the chart paper or remove all of the similar ideas except one piece of card stock as you continue this process.

When it appears that all participants are satisfied with their discussion or regrouping of the cards, distribute approximately 8–10 colored dots or stickers to each participant. Ask them to consider all of the ideas on all of the sheets of chart paper. Pose the question: "If you had to show your commitment to any of the ideas on the chart papers, where would you place your dots?" Then, have participants move to the wall and "vote" for their most powerful ideas. They may place all of their dots on one idea or distribute their votes accordingly among several ideas on several sheets of the chart paper.

After all of the dots have been posted, ask the participants to step back and consider where there is the most passion and opinion. As the group discusses each of the most powerful ideas, ask a scribe to begin creating a new sheet of chart paper, with the title: Vision Statement for the Initiative. Figure 4.5 provides a model for how the chart paper should be arranged.

Figure 4.5 Sample Vision Statement for the Initiative Chart

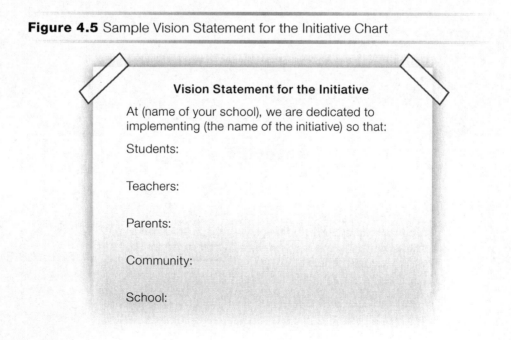

Vision Statement for the Initiative

At (name of your school), we are dedicated to implementing (the name of the initiative) so that:

Students:

Teachers:

Parents:

Community:

School:

Lift off the most powerful statements in each category (as evidenced by the dots and discussion) and have the scribe capture them in bulleted format under the appropriate category.

When completed, post the newly drafted vision statement for the initiative. Ask the participants to get into their working groups again and discuss the vision statement, pros and cons, changes they would want to see in the statement, etc. When the group appears to have consensus, ask for a "fist to five" vote (five fingers up means they support the vision wholly, and a fist means they find no merit in the vision).

Occasionally, the participants feel that the vision statement needs a little more work and is not complete. If necessary, it may be important to assign the draft to a writing team to edit and word more strongly. If the writing team is necessary, ensure that all participants receive the edited vision statement at a later date and are asked to provide their continuing feedback on the vision.

The following is a sample vision statement created by the Webster Central School District (New York) district literacy team in 2010 to propel the elementary balanced literacy initiative. Note the format, length, and complexity of the vision statement, but do not be intimidated by the length! The overall vision is likely to be lengthy as it must paint a "word picture" of what the changes will look like for each group after full institutionalization.

Webster Central Schools: Vision Statement

The Webster Central Schools are dedicated to a student centered, innovative, rigorous elementary balanced literacy program where:

Students:

- are engaged in and value literacy as a life skill;
- are known, challenged, and believed in as learners in a safe environment which values literacy;

- identify, articulate, and demonstrate the strategies of good readers and writers;

- help guide their own personal literacy achievement pathways through personal goal setting;

- interact with text at their independent levels the great majority of each school day;

- are challenged at their literacy instructional levels a portion of each school day;

- have access to engaging materials that they can read, understand, and learn from on their own; and

- use their literacy strategies in multiple contexts to learn and problem solve both in school and outside of school.

Teachers:

- demonstrate and articulate a common understanding of a comprehensive, balanced literacy program focused on student goals and outcomes;

- build on their own teaching strengths while capitalizing on student capabilities and student learning strengths;

- incorporate innovative, powerful, differentiated literacy practices in daily work with students;

- create supportive and challenging classroom cultures which immerse students in literacy and promote student risk-taking;

- effectively use professional learning communities to drive a) decisions about assessment, b) the analysis of assessment data, and c) implications for changes in instruction;

- regularly participate in high-quality, authentic, differentiated district- and school-wide professional development and implement the content and skills into daily practice; and

- nurture new and deeper partnerships with parents and community leaders to promote literacy and create supportive literacy cultures at home.

Schools and School Leaders:

- showcase literacy instruction that is differentiated, based on readiness, learning profile, and/or interest;

- guarantee clear, consistent literacy outcomes for each grade level;

- demonstrate understanding of the essential literacy outcomes for each grade level and support the alignment of these consistent outcomes across the grade levels;

- exemplify clarity of district and school literacy leadership roles and act according to those roles;

- create and sustain structures to support frequent conversations about literacy using common district language; and

- support the sustained and accessible professional literacy learning through ongoing, job-embedded, collaborative implementation of powerful, innovative practices.

Parents and Community:

- are invested in literacy partnerships among parents, schools, and the community to promote high levels of literacy;

- interact with children to support and sustain developmental literacy learning at home and in the community;

- support engagement in relevant and authentic literacy applications; and

- demand that students invest in literacy as high-performing citizens.

Developing the One-Year Operational Vision to Orchestrate the Changes

The overall vision for the initiative is critical for the reasons illustrated earlier in this chapter. Yet, as in the case of the Webster Central School District, the overall vision for the initiative will be quite extensive as it illustrates all of the changes that are expected when the initiative has been fully institutionalized.

Therefore, sometime late during the initiation stage of the change, the change maestro will be ready to reassemble his or her team to create the first-year operational vision. This operational vision statement is much shorter than the overall vision. The first-year operational vision gives the change leaders a way to "manage the horizon" (Senge 1999). The idea of a one-year operational vision (developed each year of implementation) is to give the change maestro and his or her team a way of breaking down the overall vision into more manageable "chunks" of goals. Teachers often feel overwhelmed by overall visions, seeing little chance of actualizing all of the changes illustrated in those words. But when broken down into manageable one-year visions, teachers and staff can work toward more realistic goals and changes in their practice. This idea is central to the value of the one-year vision in orchestrating the desired changes.

Senge (1999) describes this "vision horizoning" process as imagining yourself at the starting point of the initiative and looking across the horizon to the overall vision statement in the far future. This overall vision might be realistically actualized only after three to five years of implementation. Thus, to borrow from Senge's work, the change maestro's task—when just beginning the implementation phase—is to describe what this year's success looks like. This vision horizoning makes the change journey seem much shorter and more doable to the participating staff members.

The following illustrates an example of a first-year vision statement drafted by key staff members of the Greeneville City Schools (Tennessee) as they were just beginning their district-wide work in creating differentiated classrooms. The teachers, school leaders, and academic coaches all participated in extensive professional development on differentiation, and after crafting an overall vision statement, many of the same staff members came back together to begin figuring out how to "manage" the differentiation horizon, so they could meet their overall vision. After some deliberation, they created the following first-year operational vision for the changes they expected to see after one year's worth of effort and support. See if this one-year vision paints a "word picture" of the exact progress they intended to make in this year. Notice the one-year vision's length and how it paints the picture of the goals for that year.

Greeneville City Schools Differentiation Initiative First-Year Vision

To meet the needs of every student, differentiation is the unifying focus of professional learning throughout the district. Academic Coaches are facilitating professional learning on differentiation at the building level. With the support of their coaches, teachers are seen practicing differentiated instruction strategies based on their own readiness and learning. Teachers and coaches are meeting to address student learning needs and construct differentiation strategies to achieve student needs. Teacher leaders are emerging and sharing "low-prep" strategies with each other. Principals are demonstrating their commitment to and expectations for differentiation by actively communicating with other administrators, coaches, students, parents, and teachers and finding time to support differentiated practices being seen in classrooms.

Yearly Operational Vision Preparation:

- Schedule the creation of the operational vision to help "manage the horizon" sometime late in the initiation phase of the change (after the overall vision has been created).

- copies of the overall initiative vision ready for review

- chart paper

- chart stand

- chart paper divided into "placemat" design for each table group

- tape for the walls

- blank walls for posting of ideas

Orchestrating the Yearly Operational Vision Process

Participants in this short meeting will have a working knowledge of the initiative, as the first-year or one-year operational vision is developed at the end of the initiation phase of the change. Usually, by the time the first-year or one-year operational vision is developed, participations will have had professional development about the initiative and have been engaged in the planning for the initiative. In addition, participants will have helped draft an overall vision for the initiative (see previous details in this chapter). Because of all of these reasons, there will be great energy and anticipation for the creation of the first-year or one-year operational vision.

Seat participants in small tables of four to six, in a comfortable setting with walls on which to post their work. Materials should be distributed at the tables before participants arrive. Post the overall vision for easy viewing or have copies of the overall vision available for all participants.

Begin by reviewing their work in creating the vision. Ask the participants to talk about what has happened so far in the initiative. Comments will include preparations of which they are aware, the level of interest and excitement among the staff, etc. Review the overall vision and ask participants to talk about what they believe will be the major changes as a result of the initiative, as influenced by the overall vision.

Remind the participants that this overall vision cannot be achieved unless they help break it down into more manageable one-year visions to strategically guide the long-term work. Illustrate this by drawing a "vision horizon" on the chart paper. (See Figure 4.6.)

Figure 4.6 Our Vision Horizon for This Initiative

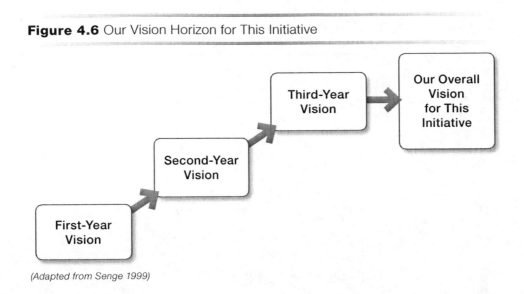

(Adapted from Senge 1999)

Using this simple graphic on the chart paper, demonstrate how the overall vision is critical, so they know when they eventually meet successful implementation. Explain how each year's vision will help all participants see what the change looks like for this year.

Ask all participants to consider the groups or structures that will be changed as a result of this initiative. To do this, direct them back to the overall vision statement and note the groups or structures listed in the statement, such as students, teachers, school, community, and/or parents. Tell the participants that they will be writing about what changes they think are reasonable for the first year of implementation, or, in other words, what will change look like after one year of the initiative. Tell them to think about these changes in terms of those same groups or structures represented in their overall vision statement. Remind them that for this year, they may not anticipate significant changes in some of the groups or structures, and this is perfectly acceptable. They are to think of the most significant changes for the most important groups or structures this year.

Distribute the chart paper placemats into those same groups represented by their overall vision statement groups or structures. Each chart paper placemat may look similar to Figure 4.7.

Figure 4.7 Typical "Placemat" Template for the First-Year Vision Process

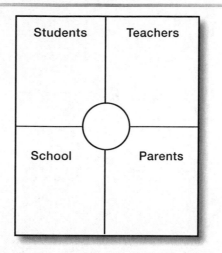

If there are five groups or structures affected by the initiative (for example, if you wanted to include the community as a group), draw the chart paper placemats into five compartments. When constructing these placemats, be sure to draw an unlabeled circle in the middle and leave plenty of space in all sections for writing. After distributing one placemat to each working table group, ask them to think about the changes they would expect to see after one year of working with the initiative. Remind them to keep in mind the overall vision and that all one-year operational visions must build to the eventual attainment of the overall vision.

Have participants at each table write directly on the placemat any change that they would expect to see for that group or structure in the year being addressed. When completed, the group participants will have written several ideas, perhaps for all or just some of the groups represented on their placemat. Then, ask the participants to lift the ideas they feel most passionate about and re-write those ideas (their best ideas) in the center circle of their placemat, one "best idea" for each group represented in the center circle.

Post all placemats from each table group and have a "docent" gallery walk, asking one person from each of the table groups to stand by his or her posted placemat and explain their ideas to all other participants as they informally walk around and review all of the placemats. When the participants appear to be finished with this gallery walk, reposition the placemats so they are side-by-side on one wall and seat participants for review and discussion of all placemats.

Facilitate the participants' discussion by highlighting one group or structure on all placemats and lifting significant changes from all placemats and writing these under the name of that group or structure on a new blank sheet of chart paper. Ask the participants to come to a consensus about the major changes they would see in this group for this particular year only, and press the participants to explain why they would think these changes are significant and necessary for the year being discussed. Reduce, eliminate, or combine the ideas for that particular affected group. When the participants appear to have a consensus, then move to the next group, and continue this process until there is consensus for an operational vision for the groups for the particular year. End this process by rewriting these intended one-year changes as a narrative, using the previous example from the Greeneville City Schools as a guide.

Be particularly cautious that the operational vision the participants write is achievable for the particular year and represents a stretch and a change, but not so massive that it cannot be accomplished. When the operational vision is completed, it will be easy for participants to see how this one-year vision will help them finally achieve the overall institutionalized vision.

Orchestrating the One-Year Vision to Point Out Short-Term Wins

Once the one-year vision has been created, the maestro is now ready to create and evaluate the actions that ensure the accomplishment of that one-year operational vision. This "action oriented" orchestrating is the heart of the leader's management of the one-year plan. After this operational vision has been defined for the specific year, consider the key staff members who will help you create the actions to fulfill your one-year vision. These key staff members may include all or some of the same participants in the one-year vision creation process defined in this chapter.

Figure 4.8 depicts how the same team in the Greeneville City Schools created their "theory of change" around their one-year operational vision. In viewing this figure, see how the one-year operational vision was centered. Note that their theory was depicted graphically in a series of sequential, critical steps. During the orchestrating of this plan, each of these steps was evaluated to see if it was accomplished and to what degree of success it achieved. In addition, each step was celebrated throughout the district, emphasizing that the move to differentiated classrooms could be manageable and successful. The district used these short-term "wins" to not only celebrate the work but also provide evidence of the change they were seeking for the first year of differentiation.

Figure 4.8 Sample One-Year Operational Vision and Theory of Change

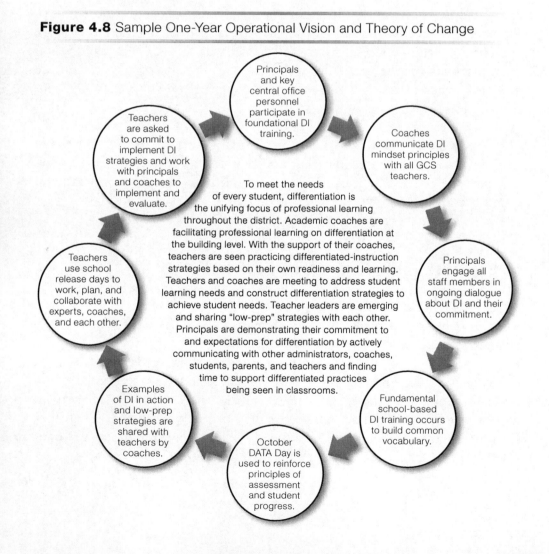

Thus, the operational one-year vision—*not* the overall initiative vision—and the action steps become the maestro's companion as he or she orchestrates the initiative from the initiation stage through implementation.

The completion of the overall vision and the one-year operational vision is critical to orchestrating the change you anticipate. Both visions give the participants an idea of the change that will signal improvement in their school. While each vision serves a different purpose, they align and work together to clearly communicate the "what" that you are trying to achieve. Remember these "big ideas" as you facilitate the creation, and orchestrate the use, of the visions to help you accelerate your progress.

Vision "Big Ideas" Reminders

The overall initiative vision is a clear word picture of what the initiative looks like when it has been fully institutionalized. It is far too extensive to be used to manage the change. For orchestrating the change, the maestro will use a succession of one-year visions. Both kinds of vision—the overall and the one-year—however, are vital to the process of implementing and institutionalizing the initiative throughout its life span.

The operational, or one-year, vision must change with every year of implementation. It signals the change that is expected for this year only and signals yearly progress to participants. Create it to manage the initiative and to evaluate progress.

The visions are as much a communication tool as they are management tools. Use the operational vision to guide your daily and weekly conversations with participants about their individual progress toward the anticipated change (see Figure 4.9).

Figure 4.9 Overall Institutional Vision

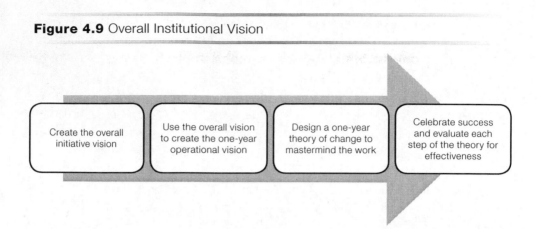

Questions for Consideration and Discussion

1. Do you have overall visions and yearly visions for your major initiatives now? If not, which initiatives need the "vision work" the most? Why?

2. Which of your initiatives are having an "implementation dip?" Why? How could the vision assist these initiatives?

3. Are any of your major initiatives fully institutionalized? What factors assisted in this long-range success?

4. Are most of your initiatives at the beginning stages and then "die a natural death" before they can be fully implemented? What can you do about it?

What Conversations Should I Be Having about This Initiative?

Chapter Four addressed the importance of having a vision for each initiative. The vision drives the work and focuses the conversations on the "right stuff" as school leaders orchestrate progress. Visions must remain vibrant and relevant as each initiative develops and becomes more institutionalized in the school's fabric. Having a vision, while critical, is hardly enough. Companion to the vision and instrumental to the success of any initiative are the *conversations* the school leaders are having with the initiative's stakeholders—parents, community leaders, district office decision makers, and, most importantly, teachers. These conversations, if successful, focus the participants on the vision and what is to be achieved.

While it can be said that the development and sustenance of the initiative's vision is a scientific, managerial action, keeping the vision alive through conversations and focusing conversations on progress requires a leader's artistry. No two conversations will ever be exactly alike, and will call on the leader to exercise minute-to-minute thinking and adjustments to simultaneously acknowledge the teacher's efforts, build the relationship, and focus on the work being achieved. Figure 5.1 illustrates this necessity.

Figure 5.1 Three Simultaneous Goals for Successful Conversations

To summarize, it is the school leader's goal to have focused conversations, while at the same time honoring practitioners' efforts and leaving the relationship better and more solid after the conversation is over. The vision serves as the focal point for the conversations.

The school leader does *not* have to sacrifice relationships if he or she is determined to get results. In fact, this chapter is undergirded by the opposite idea—that the relationship is critical to the results we must have when implementing any initiative.

Concepts and Skills in This Chapter:

- Creating conditions to motivate people
- The development of trust
- Determining practitioners' concerns as they implement the initiative
- Taking risks and dealing with resistance
- Powerful questions to ask
- The orchestration conversation framework

Three Conversation "Measures" for the Maestro's Consideration

Measure #1: Creating the Motivating Environment through Conversations

"Too many organizations—not just companies, but governments and nonprofits as well—still operate from assumptions about human potential and individual performance that are outdated, unexamined, and rooted more in folklore than in science" (Pink 2009, 9). Daniel H. Pink, in his book *Drive* (2009), elaborates by decrying school and district attempts to offer performance pay, short-term incentive plans, and other extrinsic motivators to achieve school improvement. In Pink's analysis of earlier motivation research, he quotes Edward Deci, "Human beings have an inherent tendency to seek out novelty and challenges, to extend and exercise their capacities, to explore, and to learn" (as cited in Pink 2009). Deci noted that this motivating driver, while powerful, was also quite fragile, needing a supportive environment to survive and was easily abandoned in the face of factors that whittled away at our natural, intrinsic tendencies.

Compounding this idea is the fact that school improvement is hard, complicated work. Because people need a supportive environment in which to exercise their capacities and to risk new practices, they are just as receptive to retreating from these personal challenges when the work appears to live within an "inspection" mentality. This idea may explain why so many school practitioners remark how busy they are on a daily basis but cannot really talk deeply about their progress and their students' progress—indeed, their emphasis is mistakenly on the mindless "inch deep" application of putting theory into practice.

Therefore, orchestrating an initiative into the institutionalization stage certainly is not routine. This chapter on having meaningful conversations relates squarely on having the important, tough conversations about perceived progress. Putting these principles into practice propels both school leaders and practitioners into the kinds of conversations that really matter.

Conversations must be at the soul of every organization as leaders create that environment that motivates people to explore their own creativity and take risks. Consider these important motivational concepts:

Offer Nontangible Rewards and Mean It! We know that research on student motivation emphasizes the impact that specific praise has on student performance (Brophy 2010), and the same concept applies to working with adults. Pink states that "praise and positive feedback are much less corrosive than cash and trophies" (2009, 65). Such tangible rewards may in fact focus the attention on obtaining the reward rather than attacking the problem and do not assist individuals in working toward that intrinsic satisfaction. As with students, simply noticing the effort and the production, and commenting on a) the effort and b) the potential impact has a powerful effect on motivation and attitude. The effective leader not only seeks opportunities to offer nontangible rewards but also genuinely understands the principle that people inherently want to seek out challenge and opportunities but need to do so in a relationship with the leader who believes in them and demonstrates it through his or her actions and words.

Provide Some Useful Information During the Conversation. People doing the hard business of school improvement desire and appreciate data and information. In fact, people are often comforted by information. Pink believes that people are "thirsting to learn about how they're doing, but only if the information isn't a tacit effort to manipulate their behavior" (2009, 65). The information, if it is motivational, is not general, is specific to the project or vision, and does not serve to gloss over the work or provide an ultimate compliment. In fact, the more the information is about the effort and strategy, the more effective it is. The following vignette illustrates the power of the act of providing information.

Yolanda, Information, and Motivation: A Case Study

Yolanda is a seventh-grade language arts teacher in an urban middle school. As part of the overall school improvement strategies, Yolanda's principal offered any teacher the chance to work with a district instructional coach who would work with the teacher on specific areas that the teacher wanted to improve. Then, the coach would regularly use classroom walk-through tools to gain information about the teacher's self-goals and hold a conversation about the information after each classroom visit. Yolanda was pleased to volunteer for this coaching opportunity but also a bit nervous about the information she might receive. After getting assurances from the coach and the principal about information confidentiality, she agreed to participate. After the first classroom visit and the follow-up conversation, Yolanda noticed that indeed, the coach was focusing on the goals that Yolanda had set for herself, rather than goals her principal might have set for her. She found that the coach invited her into the conversation rather than controlled it. In fact, Yolanda felt like an "equal participant" in the conversation and began to speculate on the kinds of changes she might make to get better results. As time went on and the coach finished a total of eight classroom observations, Yolanda commented to her peers that she looked forward to these classroom visits and conversations because it "is so great to get this information" and "it's allowed me to figure out how I might get better."

Give Some Autonomy to the Person! In this case study, Yolanda found that information helped propel her to make changes in her classroom. Crucial to Yolanda, however, was the idea that she felt like an equal participant in the conversation and was asked to focus on the goals she had set for herself, instead of accepting the coach's goals for her. Yolanda's success points to the power of autonomy. Pink reminds us that old-style school management focuses on the idea that people generally will wander ("happily inert") and not remain focused unless they are prodded to move forward. This idea, Pink suggests, is exactly antithetical to most human behavior and willingness to be active and engaged in the work. Differing from independence, a sense of autonomy has a motivational effect on people and their willingness to embrace challenges. Autonomy, as defined by Pink, is acting with choice, "both autonomous and happily interdependent with others" (2009, 88). Within a framework of collaboration and nonnegotiables, people strive when given autonomy over Pink's "four Ts": *Task*, *Technique*, *Team*, and *Time* (Pink 2009).

If the current culture of the school is controlling, the transition to accountable autonomy may initially be bumpy if the school leader does not support and negotiate the change from "managed" to autonomy. Conversations, then, must balance the delicate footing between prescriptive leadership to shared autonomy and accountability for results. The strategies detailed in this chapter will help the leader plan and conduct conversations that will bridge this footing.

When creating the environment and conditions for motivation, consider orchestrating the use of a) nontangible rewards, b) information, and c) autonomy within a system of leader behaviors. Simply put, when having conversations with people about the initiative, use the ideas in Figure 5.2 to plan those conversations and ask, "What should I focus on *with this person* to keep his or her motivation at high levels?" The effective school maestro will use Figure 5.2 to determine what is needed with his or her teachers to keep their motivation levels high and focused on complete institutionalization of the change.

Figure 5.2 How to Keep Motivation Levels High

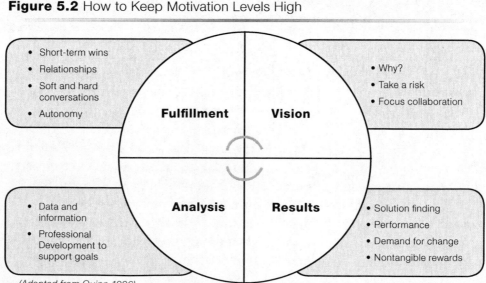

(Adapted from Quinn 1996)

Measure #2: Developing Trust for the Conversations

Patterson, Grenny, McMillan, and Switzler (2002) detail the impact that failed trust in people can have on institutionalization of an initiative. They remind us that people often assume that trust is something that you have or don't have. Either you trust someone or you don't. That puts too much pressure on trust. Trust is usually offered in degrees and is very topic or initiative specific. They suggest that the school leader deal with trust around the initiative issues, not possible trust issues with the staff person.

Think of trust and effective conversations as being directly linked. The ability to have a relationship-rich, results-focused conversation is in large part not only due to the topics being discussed, but also the amount and depth of the trust the participants of the conversation have in each other. Yet school leaders know that the idea of trust is complex. Megan Tschannen-Moran defines trust as "the willingness to be vulnerable to another based on the confidence that the other is benevolent, honest, open, reliable, and competent" (2004, 17). Understanding the importance and the interdependence among these five "facets" of trust (2004) helps the school leader model them in every conversation he or she has with teachers regarding the initiative (see Figure 5.3).

Figure 5.3 Trust Facets

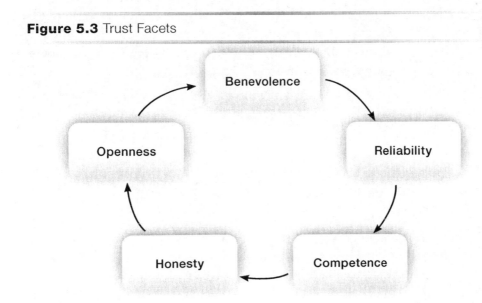

Benevolence: How can I demonstrate my goodwill and genuine concern for this person as we are discussing the initiative? As the maestro is conducting conversations about change and improvement, he or she has to make sure that he or she is perceived as an altruistic leader. "Benevolence enlivens the relationship with a sense of warmth, which generates full engagement" (Tschannen-Moran 2010, 19).

Reliability: How can I be consistent in my conversations and deeds so this teacher has confidence in me during the implementation of this initiative? Reliability is in essence predictability. Realizing that you can count on the goodwill of another to act in your best interest is powerful; conversely, if the teacher senses that the leader is a warm, well-meaning person who rarely or inconsistently comes through with commitments, reliability is breached and trust is diminished.

Competence: Does the teacher see me demonstrating the knowledge and skill to fulfill his or her expectations of me and this initiative? In the traditional sense, competence means having the "subject matter" expertise to demonstrate the effective leadership of the initiative. However, competence in orchestrating complex initiatives builds trust when the effective school maestro understands when not to give advice or suggestions, allowing the teacher to figure out his or her own ways of working more effectively. In this sense, the competent school leader understands and fully utilizes the continuum of leadership practices to demonstrate competence and build trust as seen in Figure 5.4. Armed with these considerations (or facets), look again at this graphic described in Chapter 2.

Figure 5.4 A Leader's Competence Continuum

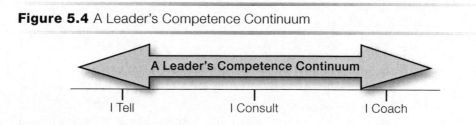

The competent school maestro weighs the various factors and demonstrates his or her competence through this range of practices. The "match" between the needs and perceptions of the teacher and the maestro's actions (from telling to coaching) builds the perception of competence among the staff implementing the initiative.

Honesty: Do the words I use in my conversations match my daily actions that all of my teachers see? Honesty "concerns a person's integrity and authenticity" (Tschannen-Moran 2010, 22). Honesty, therefore, is nothing more than the correspondence between a leader's statements and deeds. In difficult or poorly planned conversations, the school maestro may find himself or herself promising more than he or she can deliver; this action is dangerous and threatens trust by compromising honesty.

Openness: Am I remaining open to new ideas and control as I participate in this conversation? Openness is the process through which the school maestro makes himself or herself open and vulnerable to information, influence, and control (Tschannen-Moran 2010). When the school leader is open to ideas and points of view and demonstrates this in the conversation (and means it!), the teacher is more likely to demonstrate openness to new ideas as well. This "initiates an upward spiral of trust in the relationship" (Tschannen-Moran 2010).

The school maestro may use these facets to self-assess before going into any conversation with a teacher about the initiative. During the conversation, the effective leader continues to self-assess the progress of the conversation and makes adjustments based on the kind of trust that appears to be "in danger" at that moment.

The school maestro must conduct his or her conversations with teachers about the initiative in ways that maintain three simultaneous elements of trust. Consider the "formula" for the leader's thinking shown in Figure 5.5.

Figure 5.5 Formula for School Leader's Thinking

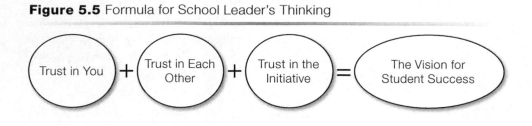

Initiative conversations must build trust in the initiative itself. By stressing the goal of the initiative, the vision for students, and by pointing out the small successes, teachers will find "faith" in the initiative's big ideas. Supporting and modeling collaboration during the conversation will encourage teachers to be more collaborative in their planning and work with fellow teachers. Finally, by modeling the five "facets of trust" in these conversations, the teachers will build deeper levels of trust in the maestro.

In addition, the effective school maestro will want to model the following dialogue behaviors during the critical initiative conversations.

Dialogue Behaviors for the Critical Initiative Conversations:

- Use open-ended questions to invite dialogue and the exploration of ideas.

- Be transparent in language so there are few misconceptions.

- Practice paraphrasing, summarizing, and clarifying as a demonstration of mindful listening.

- Assume the positive intent of the other person in the conversation.

- Be increasingly self-aware of your own actions and how the other is perceiving your words and non-verbal communication.

Measure #3: Thinking Differently about Resistance

Occasionally, the school leader will meet resistance from some of his or her staff members and be confounded by the apparent illogical and obstinate actions of them to thwart the implementation of the initiative. All effective leaders experience resistance from others as they attempt to effectively orchestrate change in their schools. Given the opportunity, leaders often want to talk about their individual cases of resistance and search for a clear "formula" to reduce the resistance in particularly toxic individuals. Staff members who resist usually have what they perceive as a good reason for their rejection of the tenets of the initiative. It could be that they have little faith or trust in the leader, little or no trust in others at the school, or little or no trust in the work they are being asked to do. Interestingly, many resisters may have good reason to resist the espoused work; indeed, they have seen initiatives come and go in their schools with little or no impact. Therefore, their resistance is their reasoned and predictable response to the maestro's request. Much to the dismay of the school leader, resisters will hold to their principles and find all sorts of ways to avoid the intent of the initiative's changes.

When creating and orchestrating conversations with staff members about school initiatives, the school leader will, then, invariably encounter resistance apparent during the dialogue. The third "measure" for that maestro to consider may be contrary to popular belief—this idea is that resistance does not need to be something to "overcome." In fact, the leader has to first understand resistance and the possible sources for the resistance if he or she is to effectively manage it. Consider two well-known authors who now think differently about resistance.

If it is really a matter of understanding resistance and coping with resistance, then the first job of the school leader is to recognize the forms of resistance that he or she may find in a school environment. Consider some of the more common manifestations of resistance in schools, shown in Figure 5.6, and begin suggestions on how to manage the different forms.

> When confronted with difficulty and uncertainty, it is natural for people to seek security and comfort of the status quo. (DuFour, DuFour and Eaker 2008, 421).

Figure 5.6 Common Manifestations of Resistance

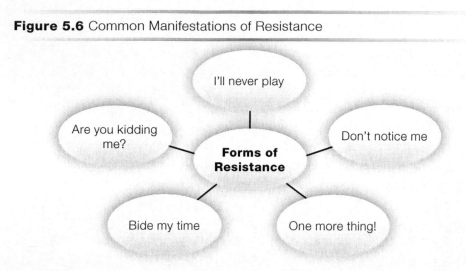

I'll never play

This can describe the most overt resister, the classic "no way" response to the initiative and the changes required to make the initiative work. The "I'll never play" resister may be hiding a fear of competence. What subtle differences in conversations may help the leader manage this form of resistance? During conversations, the effective maestro tempers his words with firm, consistent encouragement to begin the initiative with short, successful first steps.

Don't notice me

Sometimes, a resister simply doesn't want to be noticed. He or she may be overtly courteous and supportive of the maestro and school change but covertly inert in implementing any first steps. This resister is counting on the leader not noticing the lack of movement on his or her part. What subtle differences in conversations may help the leader manage this form of resistance? In discussions, the effective leader will build the relationship and encourage the resister to consider the positive changes, continuing in conversation with him or her about the purpose of the change and how to get started.

One more thing!

This resister is simply overwhelmed. The leader has asked him or her to take on one more challenge, and frankly, the staff member is not in the mood! What subtle differences in conversations may help the leader manage this form of resistance? The effective maestro, in engaging the person in discussion, breaks the change down into manageable parts and helps the resister to see how the work fits with other initiatives, simplifying the work for the resister and making those much-needed connections.

Bide my time

Knowing that initiatives historically have come and gone, this resister thinks that waiting is the smartest thing to do. Therefore, he or she simply hesitates to get started on any individual efforts to support the initiative. While not overtly negative about the initiative, he or she truly believes that waiting is the "better part of valor" and really makes sense. What subtle differences in discussions may help the leader manage this form of resistance? In conversation, the effective maestro will need to demonstrate how this initiative is different, how the initiative is at the top of the school priority list, and that beginning actions to implement the initiative are required.

Are you kidding me?

This resister believes that he or she knows better about school improvement, and openly questions the intelligence of the initiative. What subtle differences in conversation may help the leader manage this form of resistance? Carefully selecting his or her words, the effective leader must acknowledge the person's knowledge and tenure, encouraging the person to ascertain how he or she can add to the initiative's effectiveness by sharing expertise with others in how to make the initiative work better.

Spending a few minutes attempting to figure out the forms of resistance may point to approaches the effective leader may take in individualizing his or her approach to the resister. While not foolproof, an analysis of resistance form gives the effective leader some probable strategies to consider as he or she frames individual conversations with staff members to support the focused work.

An understanding of the various forms resistance may take is invaluable to the leader of the initiative. Just as important is knowledge of the reasons *behind* the resistance. If the school leader takes a few minutes to reflect on the reasons for the resistance in an honest and transparent way, he or she may gain insights about the resistance, giving him or her a possible solution to better "manage" the resistance or to simply cope with it.

Possible reasons for the resistance may be analyzed for possible leader action. Beckhard and Harris (Gallagher 2005) have written a simple but powerful formula for change leaders to use in this analysis shown in Figure 5.7.

Figure 5.7 The Resistance Formula

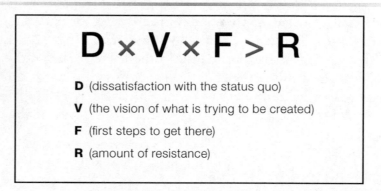

$$D \times V \times F > R$$

D (dissatisfaction with the status quo)

V (the vision of what is trying to be created)

F (first steps to get there)

R (amount of resistance)

In their formula, the product of D (dissatisfaction with the status quo), V (the vision of what is trying to be created), and F (first steps to get there) must be *greater than* the amount of resistance that people will naturally feel about the amount of labor necessary to make the initiative work. School leaders can use this formula as they develop and hold conversations with their staff members about particular initiatives. For example, if the school leader is nurturing an initiative designed to develop differentiated instruction in classrooms, he or she must create an urgency for the change through perceived dissatisfaction with the current status of instruction in classrooms, ensure that staff members understand what they are trying to accomplish (vision), and embrace and communicate short-term steps to get closer to the initiative's vision. Consider this brief case study as Bill, a school principal, begins a process to support change in mathematics instruction and, at the same time, anticipates resistance to the change.

D × V × F > R: A Case Study

Bill, a third-year principal in a rural K–5 school, prides himself on understanding his staff members. He knows that the quality of mathematics instruction in his school must improve quickly. After numerous visits to classrooms and discussions with his teachers, Bill begins to recognize that assessing and grouping students in smaller groups of instruction may lead to more accurate, timely, and focused mathematics instruction. Bill recognizes, however, that many of his teachers like their current form of whole-group math instruction and believe it is the best and most efficient way for them to cover their content. Smartly, he uses the D × V × F > R formula to plan his conversations with his staff members to accelerate change, and at the same time, reduce possible resistance to the instructional shift. Here are his personal planning notes to manage the possible resistance to this way of teaching math:

1. **D (Raise the current level of dissatisfaction with the current way of teaching mathematics in whole group):** Begin sharing data in small, grade-level teams and the best, most practical, research on differentiation and how a differentiated approach may help align small-group instruction with targeted, tailored instruction.

2. **V (What is the vision for what we are trying to create?):** Make sure that I can clearly describe what we are hoping to see in classrooms and use that language every time I'm in small groups talking about mathematics.

3. **F (First steps to make the change):** Describe my requests at first, and break the vision down into manageable first steps that are individualized with people based on their own comfort level. Ask, during small meetings, "What would be your first steps?" and then follow up with each teacher on their response.

The Gradual Release of Responsibility Model for Orchestrating Change

Could it be that resistance appears because people are not being supported to gradually assume responsibility for the change? The effective school maestro understands that a real source of resistance may relate much more to the amount and quality of work being demanded by the change, and that staff members truly believe that they have been asked to move too quickly to assign complete responsibility for the change. The idea of moving from "learning" to the independent application of the practice has, in the instructional realm, become known as the Gradual Release of Responsibility model. These concepts were originally suggested by Vygotsky and then elaborated by Pearson and Gallagher (1983). Figure 5.8 depicts the instructional model.

Figure 5.8 The Gradual Release of Responsibility Model

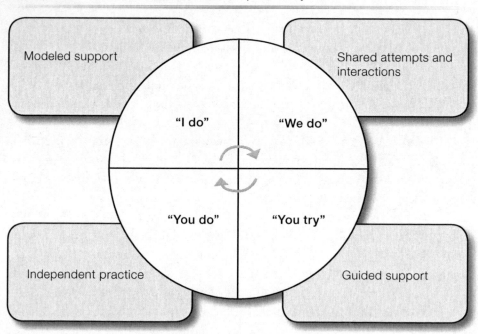

Originally designed to show the development of "mastery" a student demonstrates in applying learning independently and consistently, the Gradual Release of Responsibility is an optimal learning model in which the responsibility for task completion shifts gradually over time from the teacher to the student. This Gradual Release of Responsibility model has been foundational in reading instruction and is used to frame teaching strategies and interactions with students designed to move the student toward that independent practice of reading in varieties of contexts.

While written to illustrate student learning responsibility, the Gradual Release of Responsibility can be applied to working with adults as well. The concepts in the model can guide school leaders as they develop and hold conversations with staff members. To understand and use the Gradual Release of Responsibility model, it is first important to understand the phases or stages of the model as it relates to working with adult staff members and orchestrating and implementing the components of the initiative.

- **Modeled Support** ("I do") is the highest support for the staff member and the least amount of control for the staff member. This is the phase of learning in which the school leader initiates, models, explains, thinks aloud, and begins to develop an understanding of the major components of the initiative. Often, the "modeled support" of any initiative consists of training to learn the information about the initiative. During modeled support, the staff member is listening, learning about the initiative, and is perhaps participating or implementing a portion on a very limited basis. During modeled support, the school leader often assumes the majority of the responsibility for the initiative, and is asking the staff members to assume very little responsibility other than learning and developing positive attitudes about the initiative.

- **Shared Attempts and Interactions** ("We do") is moderate support for the staff members, and they are being asked to exercise some control over the learning. This is much like guided practice, where the school leader is still demonstrating, leading, suggesting, explaining, and responding; and the staff member is listening, interacting, and trying it out on a limited basis.

- **Guided Support** ("You try") is where the leader is handing over the responsibility a bit. There is low support for the staff member, and he or she is exercising moderate control over the implementation of the initiative components and being asked to implement them with some support from the leader. In effect, this is nearing independent practice for the staff member. The leader is watching, encouraging, clarifying, evaluating, and teaching as needed.

- In the **Independent Practice** ("You do") phase, the staff member is exercising high control and the school leader is still giving support but is not directly involved in teaching the initiative, but watching, encouraging, acknowledging, and determining additional resources to encourage the staff member to continue to implement the initiative with a great degree of autonomy.

The Gradual Release of Responsibility is a planning and diagnostic tool for the school leader as he or she evaluates the conversations about the initiative. For example, many school leaders focus their conversations in the "I do" phase—showing, telling, and explaining—and then they are disappointed when staff members might resist the change. In fact, the resistance may be due to the lack of gradual support for more independent changes in practice. When school leaders expect a huge leap from the modeled support (I do) to independent practice, they are overestimating the kind of effort many staff members feel they can take to implement the initiative. This reluctance may explain, in part, some of the resistance that leaders hear and feel—and the Gradual Release of Responsibility may explain.

The leader, then, will use the Gradual Release of Responsibility to carefully choose words to determine the kind of support individual staff members may need to progress toward more independent use of the initiative's major components. For example, early in the initiative, the leader will want to begin using words to encourage staff members to try out components of the initiative; in effect, helping them feel comfortable with a first attempt at implementation, with plenty of support from the leader. Then, if successful, the leader will want to continue to frame conversations with the staff members, supporting them to try more and deeper implementation, never removing support but altering the kind of support as he or she nurtures the movement toward independent use of the initiative in the classroom.

Putting It All Together in a Conversation Framework

How, then, can the effective school leader develop and have conversations with staff members about the work of the initiative in a way that builds the relationship, focuses on results, acknowledges effort, motivates, deepens trust, and manages resistance to the work? These goals represent a tall order! Yet it is possible. In fact, if the maestro will begin to think of conversations as being an art as well as a science, spend a few minutes analyzing possible issues *before* the conversation, and learn from the conversation, he or she will find that the conversation actually becomes the *most important vehicle* through which the leader supports the work.

Imagining the Most Exceptional Conversations

The first step in developing and having exceptional conversations about the initiative is imagining it and understanding two aspects: a) *what* the conversation is to be and b) *how* the conversation needs to happen to be most motivating and results-focused. Figure 5.9 expands the "what" and the "how."

Figure 5.9 The Exceptional Conversation

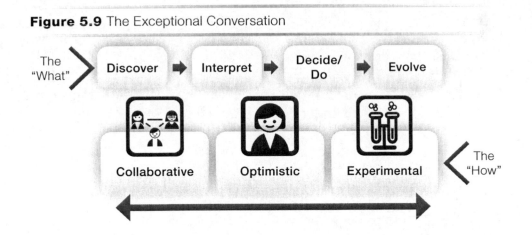

The "What": Discover → Interpret → Decide/Do → Evolve

Collaborative — Optimistic — Experimental — The "How"

The "What"

The exceptional conversation, if it supports the relationship, focuses on results, acknowledges effort, and must involve the following four sets of actions.

1. **Discover:** The conversation must invite the staff member into an exploration of current approaches and actions on his or her part.

2. **Interpret:** The school leader must invite the staff member to not only analyze current approaches and actions but interpret them in terms of impact and effects on practice and students.

3. **Decide/Do:** The conversation must invite a firm decision to try an aspect of the initiative.

4. **Evolve:** The conversation must reinforce the idea that if new actions are implemented, it will lead to an evolution in practice and a permanent adaptation of practice.

The "How"

In addition, the exceptional conversation must "feel" the following ways.

1. **Collaborative:** There must be an atmosphere of genuine collaboration and side-by-side appreciation of each other's opinions.

2. **Optimistic:** The conversation must focus on what can be done, not why issues exist. The leader must communicate a sense of support and optimism for change.

3. **Experimental:** The focus on the conversation must be on possible actions; therefore, it must demonstrate a "try it out" attitude.

The school leader may find comfort in a conversation planning framework, which can simultaneously be used as a planning tool for that important conversation as well as guidance for conducting the conversation. While the framework follows a logical sequence, it is not a recipe. Rather, it is a simple suggestion for the logical sequence and important elements of each (see Figure 5.10).

Figure 5.10 The Leader's Conversation Framework

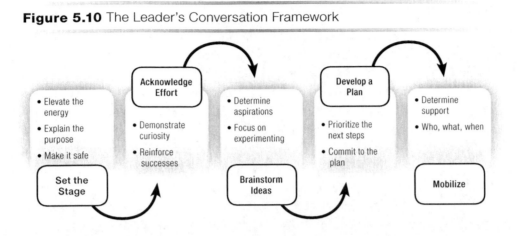

Set the Stage

At first, the leader must "elevate" the energy in the conversation, supporting the staff member, inviting his or her dialogue and ideas, and creating that optimistic climate. In addition, the leader needs to make it safe to have this conversation. As Patterson et al. (2002) remind us, because of the leader's perceived position of influence, it is often difficult to have a side-by-side conversation about the work of the initiative. In fact, the leader has to make it safe for the other person to enter the conversation and combine his or her ideas with the leader's. Part of the safety-creating process will be attained when the leader generates an energy-producing question that simultaneously focuses on the work while creating that safe climate of dialogue. Another strategy during the "set the stage" part of the conversation is the leader's explanation of the purpose of the conversation— why, in essence, are the participants meeting and focusing on this aspect of the work?

Acknowledge Effort

A leader must quickly establish a genuine curiosity for the work and the staff member's involvement in it. This curiosity can best be demonstrated through the type of questions he or she asks—open-ended questions that express the optimism about the initiative while, at the same time, gently probe the staff member's participation in the initiative. During this time, the leader must reinforce the staff member's efforts and acknowledge the effort the staff member has made to implement portions of the initiative.

Brainstorm Ideas

This part of the conversation about the work is to explore the connection the staff member is making with the work and what aspirations the staff member has about his or her involvement in the work. This "aspiration exploration" is another manifestation of the positive, optimistic nature of the conversation. Yet, notice that the school leader is squarely and firmly nurturing the conversation to include the results that he or she must have from the staff member. During the brainstorming portion of this conversation, the leader and staff member will explore all possible next steps and consider each of those steps' impact on the final vision. During this time, the leader will attempt to help the staff member explore all possibilities without settling too quickly on one effort.

Develop a Plan

When the brainstorming of ideas has occurred, the natural next step during the conversation is to develop a plan that prioritizes the actions. During the previous portion of the conversation, the leader and staff member have developed possible "next steps" and examined the implications of each. Therefore, during this phase, the commitment occurs focusing on one or two short-term steps the staff member agrees to take regarding the implementation of the initiative's work.

Mobilize

The mobilization of the conversation occurs after the plan has been made and when the staff member agrees to a spoken timeline of the action. During this phase of the conversation, the leader exchanges ideas about support he or she can give the staff member to encourage implementation, setting the tone and, if possible, a date to meet back to discuss the work.

The conversations about the initiative's work are cyclical and can be used repeatedly with staff members to help guide and troubleshoot the implementation of the initiative. When followed, the framework reinforces the important elements of the exceptional conversation as explained earlier. Simply put, the framework does not allow the conversation to veer too much from the work, while reinforcing the person and focusing on action and collaborative decisions.

As stated earlier, the quality of the conversation will be, in large part, highlighted by the quality of questions the leader asks. During the exceptional conversation, the leader will move away from "telling" and, if demonstrating genuine curiosity, move into more of a consulting or coaching role. The following are questions that can guide the conversation for each "phase" of the conversation.

Powerful Questions during the Conversation

Set the Stage

- What part of the initiative stands out for you as a shining success so far?
- What part of the work can you already celebrate?
- How are you already looking at this initiative in terms of how it can support you?
- What do you want to accomplish during this conversation about the work?

Acknowledge Effort

- It's obvious that you are working to implement the initiative in your classroom. Tell me how you are designing lessons based on the initiative and the impact you are seeing on students.
- By your enthusiasm, it's apparent that you are thinking about the components of the initiative. How are you moving from mechanical implementation to more sophisticated implementation?
- What part of the work are you the most excited about and why?

Brainstorm Ideas

- What are next steps for you that would have even more impact on your students?
- Which next step would be the most fun for you and why?
- Which ideas would push you the most? Why is that exciting?

Determine a Plan

- Which idea seems most reasonable to you?

- Where would you want to start and why?

- Which of the ideas seems like the most challenging to you?

Mobilize

- What is the best way for you to get started?

- How can I support you?

- What resources do you need?

- When do you want to get back together, so you can share your results with me?

In her orchestration of the changes at Culver Elementary School, Shirley Russell conducted many conversations with her teachers during the first year of initiation and implementation. Yet Ms. Russell's efforts focused on more "telling" than discovery and interpretation. Compounding the problem was the fact that the school had no written yearly vision of what they were to achieve in differentiation. Pockets of resistance were met head on, but Ms. Russell did not use any skill to learn the "why" of the resistance. She spent no noticeable time thinking about what would motivate her teachers to sustain their efforts. Instead, she barreled on, reminding people of the skills she expected to see and holding them accountable for it. Her conversations were not inquisitive in nature, focusing on each person's status in helping to achieve that year's vision. Instead of coaching teachers to success, she identified herself as the initiative's "flag waver." If Ms. Russell had been more strategic in the type of conversations she had, she might have learned valuable early lessons that could have prevented such an early death to her ideas.

> **Conversation "Big Ideas"**
>
> - Conversations about the work must simultaneously build the relationship, reinforce effort, and focus (demand) progress.
>
> - The school leader must have an understanding of what motivates people as he or she plans and orchestrates conversations with staff members.
>
> - Trust is crucial to productive conversations.
>
> - A conversation framework is useful for planning and delivering powerful conversations.
>
> - Questions are the school leaders' most powerful tool for creating collaborative, action-oriented conversations.

Questions for Consideration and Discussion

1. How do your conversations motivate people?

2. How is trust developed in your school? In thinking about the five trust facets, where is trust lacking? What would you do about it?

3. How do you manage resistance? What forms do you notice? Why?

4. Think of an example of an initiative that wasn't fully implemented and use the Gradual Release of Responsibility model to explain why. What would you do differently?

5. What are your best questions you use in conversations? What questions do you need to develop?

Chapter 6

How Do I Develop Targeted Professional Development to Sustain the Initiative?

Having a vision for the initiative is a huge tool for the maestro, as it guides the kinds of relationship-rich, results-focused conversations that must take place during the years of implementation. Also significant to the school leader is how people learn the knowledge and skills in order to implement the changes. Professional development conjures up mental images in many teachers and school leaders. Some of those images are not necessarily positive. Ask around, and the effective school leader will find that much of professional development seems misguided, unfocused, bloated at the beginning of the initiative, and not created or orchestrated to maintain the energy and skill needed to institutionalize the change.

This is a conundrum to the school leaders. We know that targeted adult learning is vital to the implementation of any initiative. At the same time, we often design and implement it poorly! Beautifully crafted and carefully managed, professional development can at once be energizing, coalescing, and gratifying. Indeed, it can be exactly the "just in time" punch that teachers need to continue to implement necessary changes—provided the professional development has been designed with long-term sustenance in mind.

Consider the concept addressed in Chapter Four—detailing the life span of the initiative. In that chapter, we outlined that life span as being in three distinct but interrelated phases: Initiation, Implementation, and Institutionalization. Figure 6.1 summarizes those changes. Notice the addition of adult learning to the scheme.

Figure 6.1 The Life Span of a School Initiative

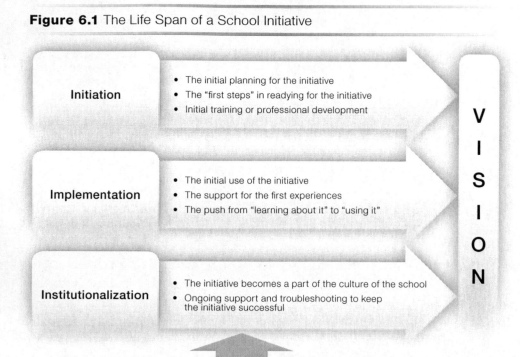

Initiation
- The initial planning for the initiative
- The "first steps" in readying for the initiative
- Initial training or professional development

Implementation
- The initial use of the initiative
- The support for the first experiences
- The push from "learning about it" to "using it"

Institutionalization
- The initiative becomes a part of the culture of the school
- Ongoing support and troubleshooting to keep the initiative successful

V I S I O N

Professional Development

Professional development is the foundation on which the life span of the initiative rests. The school leader must know and be committed to the exact content, process, and context of professional development that is needed at this moment in time to move the initiative forward—at any point in the initiative's life span and throughout the work until the change is fully institutionalized.

Concepts and Skills in This Chapter:

- Standards for quality professional development
- Powerful, school-based professional development designs that work
- Building in daily learning to support the initiative
- Gradually releasing the responsibility to teachers to apply their learning
- Coalescing school teams around learning to sustain the initiative

The Standards for Professional Development

In 2011, Learning Forward, an international organization dedicated to quality professional development, published the Standards for Professional Learning. Calling it "professional learning" instead of professional development, the organization wished to redirect the focus to efforts educators make in their continuous improvement, placing importance on the idea of adult learning more than ever before. For our purposes, we will continue to call it professional development because the term is still most recognized in the field. Figure 6.2 illustrates their premise behind the power of professional development (Learning Forward 2011).

Figure 6.2 Professional Learning

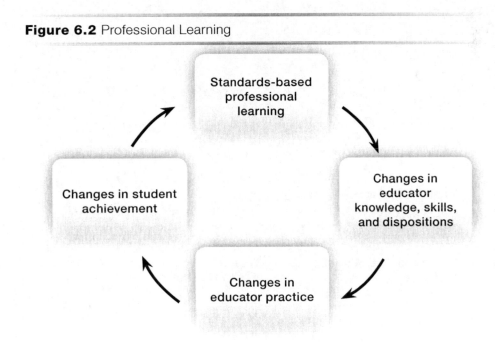

The leader's goal in designing and delivering professional development, then, is to ensure that the professional development will focus on changes in learning and application, so students will benefit.

As stated in the report "Teaching the Teachers" from the Center for Public Education, research suggests that the instruction needed to prepare students for college and 21st century careers is not the instruction most teachers currently use in their practice. In other words, teacher learning is the linchpin between the present day and the new academic goals. Merely keeping students working bell to bell is not enough; teachers have to learn new ways to teach, ways to teach they likely never experienced themselves and that they rarely see their colleagues engage in. Creating this type of teacher development is one of the biggest challenges school districts face today. Professional development in an era of accountability requires a change in a teacher's practice that leads to increases in student learning. The Center for Public Education report on professional development finds that for teachers to successfully change an instructional practice, they must try it 20 times. When a new strategy is not immediately successful, teachers are not guaranteed to use it again unless they have support. Coaching is the best way to ensure that these necessary shifts are being implemented, reflected upon, supported, and tried again until it becomes a regular part of a teacher's practice (Gulamhussein 2013).

Learning Forward's Standards for Professional Learning function in concert with each other to help educators increase their own effectiveness so students will achieve more. The seven Learning Forward standards are listed in Figure 6.3 (Learning Forward 2011):

Figure 6.3 Standards for Professional Learning

Standards for Professional Learning	Core Elements of Each Standard
Learning Communities: Professional learning that increases educator effectiveness and results for all students occurs within learning communities committed to continuous improvement, collective responsibility, and goal alignment.	A cycle of continuous improvement is inherent in all teams. Members of the team have collective responsibility and act on it. Members hold each other accountable for actions and results.
Leadership: Professional learning that increases educator effectiveness and results for all students requires skillful leaders who develop capacity, advocate, and create support systems for professional learning.	School leaders advocate and plan for high-quality professional development. Leaders create ways to support the long-term professional development to support the initiative. School leaders model their own learning for their teachers and staff.

Standards for Professional Learning	Core Elements of Each Standard
Resources: Professional learning that increases educator effectiveness and results for all students requires prioritizing, monitoring, and coordinating resources for educator learning.	Leaders must prioritize all of the resources available, including time, human, fiscal, material, and technology—in order to support the initiative over time. Leaders must also coordinate resources, to ensure that the right resources are being supplied to the needs of the initiative.
Data: Professional learning that increases educator effectiveness and results for all students uses a variety of sources and types of student, educator, and system data to plan, assess, and evaluate professional learning.	School leaders have to find access to all forms of data, including student performance data, teacher data, and overall system data, and put these data in the hands of teachers to analyze learning and performance. The evaluation of professional development must be ongoing, using data which demonstrate levels of evaluation ranging from learning, to application, to performance.
Learning Designs: Professional learning that increases educator effectiveness and results for all students integrates theories, research, and models of human learning to achieve its intended outcomes.	There are multiple models for professional development that can work effectively in schools. The learning designs (models) must be carefully selected and managed to promote long-lasting adult engagement.
Implementation: Professional learning that increases educator effectiveness and results for all students applies research on change and sustains support for implementation of professional learning for long-term change.	School leaders must know and understand how change occurs and apply those concepts at their schools. Implementation must be sustained over time.
Outcomes: Professional learning that increases educator effectiveness and results for all students aligns its outcomes with educator performance and student curriculum standards.	Professional development must be standards-based. School leaders must ascertain how the professional learning is aligned with not only educator evaluation performance standards but also student learning and curriculum standards.

(Adapted from Learning Forward 2011)

The effective school leader understands that all seven of these standards must be fully in place in order for educators within the school to reach their full learning potential. These standards, then, describe the attributes of effective professional development that must drive the initiative toward full institutionalization. These standards may be used by the effective school maestro to not only design but also orchestrate high-quality professional development that sustains the initiative over time. School leaders should regularly review and use the standards as a planning and management template for their professional development in their schools.

School-Based Professional Development Designs That Work

There are numerous factors that influence the design (what it looks like) of professional development at schools. These factors include the goals of the learning, the amount of trust and collaboration among the adult learners, their familiarity with the content of the professional development, the urgency and the magnitude of the change, and the resources, to name a few of the most important. Consider the factors and the questions shown in Figure 6.4.

Figure 6.4 Factors That Influence Professional Development Design

Factors	Questions Raised
Goals	• Knowledge? • Awareness? • Practice? • Reflection?
Trust and Collaboration	• Trust among the staff? • Trust with the leadership? • Trust in the work?
Content Familiarity	• Readiness of the staff? • "Distance" from the practice?

Factors	Questions Raised
Urgency	• How critical is the change viewed? • How much time can be spent on implementing the change?
Resources	• Time? • Funding? • Access to materials?

For example, if the goal for the proposed professional development is knowledge about a new practice, the initiative is at its first beginning stages of work. The staff members are ready for the change in terms of their own knowledge level, and there is some urgency to get the new knowledge to the teachers. In these instances, training is a viable professional development model and may be the best design for the adult learning (and most efficient, in terms of expended resources). However, if there is a high amount of trust and collaboration among staff members and they have a history of working together on problems and learning, training may not capitalize on these contextual elements. This may be especially true if the initiative is in full implementation; as during full implementation, training often does not address the kinds of management and practical issues that teachers desire when in full throes of work in the change. In these circumstances, other professional learning designs may be desired, especially those designs that put teachers in informal groups to learn, set their own goals, and hold each other accountable for implementation and sharing of results from their classrooms. The following table develops some effective designs for professional development (Gordon 2004; Joyce and Calhoun 2010; Learning Forward 2011). No single design for professional development is better than another—it depends on the circumstances, goals, and the factors fully described earlier. The school maestro must carefully weigh the five factors mentioned in Figure 6.4 and then select the model that seems best suited for results at his or her school at the particular time of the initiative's life span shown in Figure 6.5.

Figure 6.5 Several Effective Professional Development Designs

Professional Development Design	Description	Factors to Consider
Training, Courses, Seminars	Highly structured PD far removed from the classroom context, selected when it is determined that a large number of staff members need to learn from an "expert" to quickly gain knowledge or awareness.	• The urgency of the change and necessity of quick acquisition of knowledge and/or awareness • The need for application of practice • Training is not necessarily linked to actual application of practice • The plan to support the application of practice after the training
Immersion	An inquiry-based design in which teachers are "immersed" in the activities they would be asking students to fulfill. Typically, immersion is accomplished at schools where teachers work through materials, kits, and textbooks together, creating and experiencing the same kinds of assignments and activities they will ask students to perform. Immersion is useful for gaining knowledge, awareness, and providing reflection time.	• Time for teacher collaboration and practice • The commitment teachers have to application • Trust among the teachers • Support for resources to focus the immersion
Curriculum Development and Implementation	Teachers working together to either develop new lesson plans or strengthen/revise previous practice. Curriculum development is useful for developing new knowledge about a content area and providing practice for implementation of the new plans within a collegial setting.	• Time for curriculum development, discussion, and implementation • Ongoing support for application • Trust and history of communication and dialogue among the practicing teachers • The extent of problem solving that teachers must accomplish and the practicality of their demands
Analyzing Student Work	Examining samples of student work and products in order to understand students' thinking and learning strategies around an idea or concept. The study of the work leads to further decisions about appropriate teaching strategies, re-teaching, and materials selection. Design is particularly effective in supporting reflection, new knowledge, and awareness.	• Commitment to a unified assignment and the selection of work samples to review • Trust and history of communication and commitment to experimenting with new strategies • Time for review and conversation • Whether or not the initiative is in full implementation

Professional Development Design	Description	Factors to Consider
Case Analyses	Case analyses can include case studies, video clips, etc. The examination presents a real-life scenario in which teacher practice is discussed and deliberated, with implications in terms of issues or outcomes. Case analyses are effective for reflection and the acquisition of knowledge.	• Materials and resources for cases • Time for extended review and conversations • Trust and history of communication skills among the participating teachers
Mentoring and Coaching	Usually one-on-one with equally or sometimes more experienced teacher to improve teaching and learning through feedback, observation and conversation, problem solving, and/or co-planning. Mentoring and coaching are particularly effective when the goal includes practice, knowledge, and/or reflection.	• Human resources • The levels of trust throughout the organization • A history of conversation and problem solving • Peer-to-peer collaboration and comfort
Study Groups and Book Studies	Related study groups and book studies involve small groups in regular, structured, and collaborative interactions regarding topics identified by the group and/or by the book/resource being used. Book studies are particularly useful for awareness and knowledge. Study groups have a bias toward implementation of new practice after the learning; therefore, they are useful if the goal for professional development includes knowledge, awareness, practice, and/ or reflection.	• Fiscal resources for the materials to be examined and studied • Time for study and collaboration • Trust among staff members • History of peer-to-peer work
Action Research	A close cousin to study groups and book studies, action research is known by many titles. Disciplined action research involves locating a problem area in student learning, collecting data about the problem, studying relevant resources, deciding to take action, and then studying the results in terms of future action or decision making. Action research is particularly useful for knowledge, practice, and reflection.	• History of peer-to-peer work • Trust among sharing of practice • Time for study and collaboration • Relevant when the initiative is in full implementation

Let's consider the Initiation/Implementation/Institutionalization life span again. The selection of the appropriate professional development design depends on so many factors, the most important factor being the life stage of the initiative. Whether or not the initiative is at the beginning stages, full implementation, or the beginning of institutionalization has a direct bearing on the kind of content selected for the professional development, the consideration of the cultural and contextual factors with the school and staff, and the selection of the right design for the professional development to reach the learning's full potential for application and impact. Investigate the following case study as an illustration of these points.

Differentiation and Fry Elementary School: A Quick Case for Discussion

The staff at Fry Elementary School spent time in an end-of-the year meeting in May, examining student performance data, which revealed significant gaps in student achievement among their 3rd, 4th, and 5th graders in reading and mathematics. Their discussion of student "gap closure" led them to review possible instructional causes for the lack of performance. By the end of the meeting, the teachers generally agreed that they should spend more time on differentiated instructional strategies, grouping strategies for students, and formative assessment. Since they were at the "initiation" stage of this major change, they decided that training was needed in these three areas. Armed with great enthusiasm, they engaged in training over three days in August, each day on one of the three topics. The goal for this training was awareness and new knowledge. The principal asked teachers to submit "tickets out the door" after each day of training, detailing what they have learned and their attitudes toward the training.

Once school started, the principal and her team realized that they needed to support teachers for making small changes in either their instructional strategies, grouping students, or assessing students. They determined that at the beginning of this implementation stage, training would not be the best design. Based on the kind of positive culture prevalent in the school, the willingness of teachers to work together and discuss what they are learning, and the need to gently press them into applying what they had learned, the principal and her team determined that she would implement study groups—disciplined small groups of teachers who agree to meet about one specific topic and implement strategies they are learning, and bring results back for further discussion and further action. She asked all of her teachers to select among the three study groups—differentiation strategies, grouping, and assessment. Teachers selected their groups and in November, began meeting twice a month after school (instead of faculty meetings) to begin their implementation work.

Building in Daily Learning to Support the Initiative

As you can infer from this case study, the principal was thoughtful in her professional development design. She knew that training was important at first, or during the initiation phase. Yet she also realized that as they moved closer and closer to actual implementation of the work, she needed more informal, collegial strategies to support her teachers as she gently moved them from "learning" to "doing." This flexibility and "matching" of the design to the eventual goal of implementation is critical for the school maestro. Professional development will only work if it is seen as an integral part of the initiative, not periodic "events" that pull teachers away from their work. Indeed, professional development must be seen as "job embedded," occurring as close to the teacher's workday and work elements as possible. Creating this invigorating operational definition of professional development requires effort on the part of the school maestro. In orchestrating change throughout the life span of the initiative, consider these suggestions for creating the time and opportunity for teachers to continually talk about, implement, and share the results of their work.

Talk about the work

School maestros should change the content of their daily informal conversations. Instead of only exchanging pleasantries about the day, it is important to not only have these "soft" conversations but also ask about the work and how it is going with the teacher (the hard stuff). Finding one to two minutes to have these conversations with several teachers each day, the leader can continue to keep a pulse on the change and how it is proceeding. He or she will also learn a lot about the problems teachers are having and will be better able to match a response with the kind of problem being heard. These short, informal conversations are a great way to reinforce the overall vision for the work and the purpose behind the present press to apply what is being learned.

Find time

Time is often viewed as the most critical hindrance to the focus and the work teachers must do together regarding the initiative. The effective leader masterminds opportunities to find time for teachers to work together. Such opportunities may include: reducing the number of required faculty meetings and, instead, delivering faculty meeting information through technology or print; covering class time for teachers periodically, so groups can meet within the school day to share their implementation ideas; using early release days or school-level professional development days for small informal work among teachers instead of in-service.

Check on resources

Resources are often front-loaded at the beginning of the initiative and at the beginning of professional development. A survey of the needed resources is often more critical *after* this initial period, when teachers are being asked to implement what they have learned. To put it another way, it is often during the beginning implementation phase that teachers realize the resources they really need for their work. They must be able to communicate this need and receive the support if they are to move beyond the initial excitement of initiation and into the hard work of making it happen.

Point out small wins

When pressed to begin applying what they have learned in professional development, teachers are motivated by acknowledgement, purpose, and above all, a sense of mastery. Mastering large-scale changes such as the move toward grouping, differentiated learning, or informal assessment strategies requires the maestro to break what appear to be massive changes into more manageable "chunks" of application that allow teachers to experience mastery of these smaller skills as they continue to aim for the overall vision. Therefore, daily adult learning should focus on these small steps, the "what's next for us" conversations, so the overall vision is over several years of the "horizons" that Chapter Four addresses.

Gradually Releasing the Responsibility for Teacher Application of Their Learning

In professional development, the goal is not just adult learning. As stated before, the goal is that the adults in the school implement their knowledge and skills in ways that positively affect students. Read the following scenario, consider the professional development plan, and answer this question: "Why didn't they get to implementation?"

Why Didn't We Get to Implementation?

Mary Salvans, the principal at a respected elementary school, has determined with her team that training is needed at the beginning of the year to provide her teachers with the awareness and knowledge of new reading strategies to augment their instruction. Charged with enthusiasm, she is excited to see her teachers respond to the training in August. Their feedback is uniformly positive, and they seem poised to begin implementing grouping strategies, formative assessment, and rigorous independent work, some of the major concepts in the training. Salvans can't wait to get into classrooms and begin to see signs of this implementation. She continues to have conversations about the reading training and waits until October to get into classrooms to see the implementation. To her dismay, however, when she does visit classrooms, she sees little signs of the training put into practice.

Do you remember Shirley Russell, our principal at Culver Elementary School? In spite of her best efforts and three days of carefully planned professional development, she yielded few results by the end of the first year. Doesn't Mary Salvans's case sound too much like the case for Shirley Russell and Culver Elementary School? Just like the dilemma that Ms. Russell faced, Ms. Salvans thought she had crafted a good plan for her professional development. Yet, to her dismay, she experienced the same disappointment that Ms. Russell observed as both of them were pressing for implementation. In effect, there were few changes noticed and yet thousands of dollars had been invested in the changes!

There is probably a logical, while unsettling, explanation for the lack of implementation of practices with Ms. Salvans's teachers. We know that training, while productive for acquiring awareness and knowledge, is notoriously ineffective for implementation (Killion et al. 2012). Additionally, we know that the teachers in this case were asked to make a rather broad leap from the acquisition of new knowledge, and perhaps new skills, to implementation within a matter of weeks. Again, the Gradual Release of Responsibility model, first introduced in Chapter Five (Pearson and Gallagher 1983), becomes important to the school maestro. Remember that this model illustrates how students come to independent mastery of skills; yet it also unveils a common picture and warnings about adult learning. To put it another way, the model provides the school maestro not only a template by which to gauge failed professional development but also, and more importantly, a guiding tool to use when planning effective professional development for the life span of the initiative. Consider again the four quadrants of gradual release (see Figure 5.8).

In effect, Ms. Salvans's school participated in "modeled support," the "I do" or "I show you" design of professional development, where someone who is viewed as an expert provides training to teachers who are in need of new awareness and knowledge. Usually presented away from the classroom context, and in most cases physically away from the school, training provides a great example of an initial foray into professional development designed to spark the change in practice. However, if training is not coupled with more job-embedded professional development designs targeting small groups of teachers working together to implement their learning, the best intentions for change will certainly fail. In other words, Ms. Salvans's school needed more. After the initial training, the teachers needed time to begin writing lesson plans that incorporated their learning about grouping, assessment, and independent work. With none provided, the pressures of daily practice won over and teachers resorted to more comfortable practices. The Gradual Release of Responsibility model also points out that if adults are to embrace the new practices on a routine basis, they will need guided support, the "you try" forms of professional development, through coaching, mentoring, co-teaching, and the mastery of small practices that are the building blocks to the overall changes sought in the vision. In essence, Ms. Salvans neglected what she knew about the way children and adults acquire independence in applying new skills.

If we could turn back time, this is the way Ms. Salvans might orchestrate the professional development regarding new reading practices in her elementary school.

Turning Back the Clock: Mary Salvans's Professional Development Plan

Mary Salvans, the principal at a respected elementary school, has determined with her team that training is needed at the beginning of the year to provide her teachers with the awareness and knowledge of new reading strategies to augment their instruction ("I Do" or "I Show"). Charged with enthusiasm, she is excited to see her teachers respond to the training in August. Their feedback is uniformly positive and they seem poised to begin implementing grouping strategies, formative assessment, and rigorous independent work—some of the major concepts in the training. Principal Salvans can't wait to get into classrooms and begin to see signs of this implementation.

In early September, after the start of school, Ms. Salvans began routinely finding time for her teams of teachers to get together and discuss what they learned about grouping, assessment, and independent work. During these hour-long planning times once a week, Ms. Salvans asked the teachers to concentrate on reading for their discussion and encouraged them to collaboratively plan a strategy they had learned that they felt would positively impact their students ("We Do"). Principal Salvans regularly sat in on these grade-level planning meetings and was pleased to see the teams use this time to efficiently plan and commit to a new practice in their classrooms. She asked them to work together to bring back samples of student work after their implementation for further discussion and deliberation.

In early October, Ms. Salvans discussed the reading work with her faculty during a regular faculty meeting. She encouraged her teachers to continue to take risks and try out other practices that they had learned in training and had discussed during their grade-level meetings. In addition, she told them that she was going to begin to look at reading during her walk-through visits and specifically wanted to see how they were incorporating grouping strategies ("You Try"). Seizing the chance now to visit classrooms, Ms. Salvans got into as many as possible during a three-week period and provided individual feedback to each teacher during short follow-up conversations, focusing on the grouping that she had seen and the perceived effectiveness of the grouping. She now plans on targeting independent work for her next round of walk-through observations, and has told her teachers that this will be the focus when she is in their classrooms in November.

Salvans's design for professional development has more of a chance to succeed because she is aware of the Gradual Release of Responsibility model and understands how adults, as well as students, respond to the carefully orchestrated shifting of responsibility to the teacher for implementation of practice.

Using Teams to Support Ongoing Learning and Implementation

As pointed out in the Gradual Release of Responsibility model, the "We Do" concept is critical for moving people from static learning to the beginning of implementation. Principal Salvans's new design for her school capitalized on the "we do" phase and the power of her teams to support each other for experimentation. This portion of her design worked because her grade-level teams already had a culture for dialogue and collaboration. They also had a certain amount of trust among each other. (See Chapter Five for more on trust.) But what does the school leader do when he or she senses that the culture to support team learning is not as deep or as much a part of daily activity as needed to support ongoing adult learning, experimentation, and implementation of ideas? In these cases, it makes sense for the school maestro to spend regular time getting teams "ready" for collaboration, exploration of ideas, and supported implementation of new practices. Use the following as a checklist and guide for the construction of "learning teams" (Love [ed] 2009; DuFour, DuFour, and Eaker 2008; Walsh and Sattes 2010).

Make sure teams of teachers have a collective purpose, vision, and clear directions. The teachers on the team must understand how their work together fits into the overall sequence of professional development and what they are to accomplish. Much of this will be made clear if the maestro has managed the creation of a yearly vision (see Chapter Four) that clearly articulates what they are to achieve this year in terms of the initiative. If teachers clearly understand the vision for the initiative, then they can make collective commitments that clarify what each teacher will do on the team to contribute to that vision. The maestro must be careful not to assume that the teams of teachers know their purpose when they get together to talk about their work, share ideas for implementation of strategies they have been learning, and/or look at student work to see the results of their labors. Face-to-face conversations by the maestro with each school team will ensure that clarity is held by all.

Emphasize that teams must have a bias for action. The emphasis for teams should not be so much on talking about their learning as doing something with it. Indeed, as DuFour, DuFour, and Eaker (2008) remind us, teachers view the most powerful professional learning as within the context of action, and they really value collective experience. The maestro, then, orchestrates conversations with all of his or her teacher teams, focusing questions on the results they are getting (see Chapter Five). This subtle direction to the bias for action will force success to be based on implementation and results, instead of the often stagnant talk that seems to identify some teacher teams.

Ensure teachers know their roles in the team. Teachers are often called to come together to process and implement strategies they have been learning, and yet, when in team meetings, they seem to flounder and express frustration with the process. Part of the issue may be in role definition.

While most team members view themselves as "equals," there are subtle leadership roles within the teams that may be important in ensuring the development of healthy team learning and implementation processes. At first, the school maestro may determine that he or she must serve as the "lead" in a team, but that role will need to be quickly shifted to either one member or several members of the team itself. When the team is called on to process and begin implementing the ideas they are learning, it will be comforting for the team if the maestro is specific in identifying not only the purpose and vision for the team, but what they are to produce, and how it will be led. Even teachers who are not serving to "lead" the conversation have roles to fill in terms of their participation and assistance. Norms will help to identify these important roles.

Prioritize time for conversation, collaboration, and implementation. As Nancy Love (2009) reminds us, teaching occurs in three parts—planning, doing, and reflecting. We traditionally think, however, that if the teacher is not in front of the students, he or she is somehow not doing his or her job! The effective maestro, then, will understand the importance of creating time for teachers within the school day for reflection on their practices and conversation about implementation of the new ideas they are learning with each other. Love (2009) recommends at least 45 minutes per week of uninterrupted, protected time for conversation and collaboration around implementation. Her ideas of finding time for teams to learn and work together include the following:

Finding Time for Teams to Learn and Work

- Buy time
- Hire substitutes to release teachers
- "Cover" class time for teachers with volunteers, instructional aides, etc.
- Make time
- Start school late or end early periodically
- Use common planning time once a week for adult learning, collaboration, and implementation
- Rethink time
- Release teams of teachers from lunch or recess duty

- Review funding sources and use available funds to hire assistance to cover teachers

- Regroup students to release teachers

Professional Development "Big Ideas"

- ✌ Professional development must be viewed in terms of the life span of the initiative. Different stages call for different professional-development strategies.

- ✌ Worthy professional development must be connected to the overall vision and the achievement sought for students.

- ✌ Many professional development initiatives are "front-loaded" and fail in the second or third years because there is no support for implementation.

- ✌ The Gradual Release of Responsibility model must be used as school leaders orchestrate the changes desired.

- ✌ School leaders must work to build teams of teachers for collaboration and implementation.

Questions for Consideration and Discussion

1. Have you ever experimented with another professional development design other than training? How did it work? What were the results?

2. Could you use the Gradual Release of Responsibility model to explain why a professional development initiative either succeeded or failed? What happened? Why?

3. How do you find time for collaboration within the school day? What have been the results?

4. How have you served as the leader of professional development in your school?

5. Are your teams ready for collaboration and implementation? If so, how do you know? If not, what do they need?

How Do I Know if Anything Is Changing as a Result of This Work?

Culver Elementary School was deep in the process of implementing the changes, and yet Shirley Russell really didn't know how to describe what was going on. In her limited leadership experience, the implementation of the practices was going as planned. Yet, well into her first year of implementation, Ms. Russell was surprised to find out that teachers were resisting the changes and, in effect, not changing their practices much at all. Principal Russell approached her teachers in a rather one-dimensional way, prodding them to implement the changes or reminding the reluctant ones of her expectations. We have no evidence that Ms. Russell ever asked her teachers about their concerns or really tried to describe the nature of the varying degrees of implementation. Principal Russell was certainly busy in promoting the changes, so we cannot criticize her efforts in terms of her energy and enthusiasm for the changes. What was missing was an ongoing evaluation of the efforts to see what specifically was changing along the life span of the initiative.

Orchestrating the work of an initiative in schools is hard enough. So the school leader reading this will probably not ask the question, "Do I really have to evaluate it?" The answer, thankfully, is a resounding yes! Consider this. Prior to this, the evaluation of an initiative has traditionally rested on two common areas of interest: 1) whether or not people were excited about the work, and 2) whether or not the work resulted in student performance. Figure 7.1 shows the balance between the two common areas.

Figure 7.1 Traditional Evaluation Measures

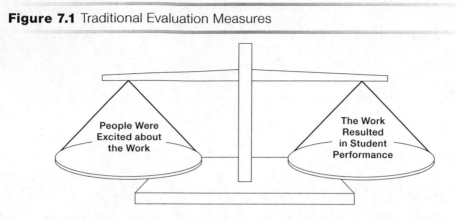

The problem with these two common areas of program evaluation is that they are not sufficient alone and do not give the maestro useful information to use as he or she is managing the initiative. In a sense, both of those traditional evaluation sets of data are "terminal." One area, whether or not people were excited, is generally a measure of how people are reacting to the initiative. These data are particularly useful at the beginning of the work. The other area of traditional evaluation is student performance, which can usually be measured only at the full implementation of the initiative. In other words, following this traditional method of evaluating your initiative will yield *no* data that can guide you while you are in the middle of the work, moving toward full implementation. The question, therefore, is this: "Are there ways to effectively measure the initiative at *all* stages of its life span? If so, what are they?"

The school leader is now fully equipped to tackle these questions. We have worked on the importance of the vision as a guide for the work and have examined yearly visions as the goals by which the maestro can measure

Concepts and Skills in This Chapter:

- The case for evaluation and the common mistakes leaders make
- The Evidence-Interpretation-Action cycle for leaders to use
- "Levels" of evaluation to guide the assessment of progress
- Assessing reactions and concerns—using the Stages of Concern
- Assessing teacher behavior changes—using the Levels of Use
- Using the information to direct the maestro's actions

the impact on teachers, students, and the school. We have also spent time with professional development practices and strategies that work along the life span of the initiative. The maestro has also studied dialogue strategies and has developed ways to hold conversations with teachers about the initiative. This chapter, therefore, helps the maestro put the work together in an evaluation sequence that can guide his or her daily actions, gathering evidence along the way to help the maestro alter his or her actions to get accelerated and deeper results. In essence, this chapter is about the maestro using the yearly vision to establish clear goals for each year, developing learning around the vision, keeping the initiative alive through daily conversations, and gathering information in easy and useful ways to help him or her know, at any given time, how successful the work is.

The Mistakes We Often Make when Evaluating Our Big Initiatives

So many times, the school leader will launch an initiative, front load his or her efforts in terms of huge amounts of professional development and resources in the early stages of initiation, and then simply "hope" that things will go well. What is so critically important is knowing, along the way, whether or not the initiative is working and meeting its yearly goals. Faced with the question from his or her supervisor "How is that initiative going?", the school leader may be forced to respond with soft, meaningless descriptions of what is going on—not really evaluations of the work, instead, the documentation and tallying of what was done, not how effective it is (Guskey 2000).

Secondly, most evaluations of critical work in schools are way too shallow and narrow. Consider professional development actions, for example. Most professional development evaluation surveys focus on whether or not the participants reacted favorably to the content and process in the session, not more important indicators of behavior change, implementation, and impact. It is as though we are not concerned with those measures, which is remarkable because they are real indicators of whether or not the initial positive reactions to the professional development *lead to anything*, which is what we really ought to be measuring.

Whether or not your efforts and support really lead to changes in the classroom is the question we should be answering. In order to do this, evaluations of all important initiatives must be committed to the "long haul" of the work—recognizing, as we have said before, that an initiative has a life span, and that it will take years to get changes fully institutionalized. We must know how each initiative is doing at any given point in its life—beginning, middle, and end. Knowing this information allows the school leader to adjust his or her support of the initiative and recognize the fact that initiatives need very different kinds of support in the third or fourth years of existence than they did in the initial year of work.

Consider these ideas and questions before reading on:

Think about one important initiative that is going on in your school or school district:

- What is the current success of that initiative?

- How would you describe the success of the initiative in terms of your teachers, students, and school?

- How do you know, without a doubt, that your description is accurate?

- What is next for you, in terms of this initiative? What is your next set of supports to move the initiative along? Why are those the right actions?

The Evidence-Interpretation-Action Cycle

The previous questions just described the kind of cyclical thinking that must occur with maestros as they lead the work. In essence, the questions frame the Evidence-Interpretation-Action cycle that must be incorporated by leaders as they evaluate the progress of the initiative and consider new actions to support the work as it develops in deeper ways in the schools. This cycle becomes the single most important series of continuous actions the leader takes to seamlessly weave together his or her actions, the gathering of evaluation evidence, and the interpretation of that evidence that leads to new, more finely honed actions on the leader's part. Review Figure 7.2 and the explanations of each component before we explore when and how to use this cycle of evaluation, and work with your most important initiatives.

Figure 7.2 Evidence-Interpretation-Action Cycle

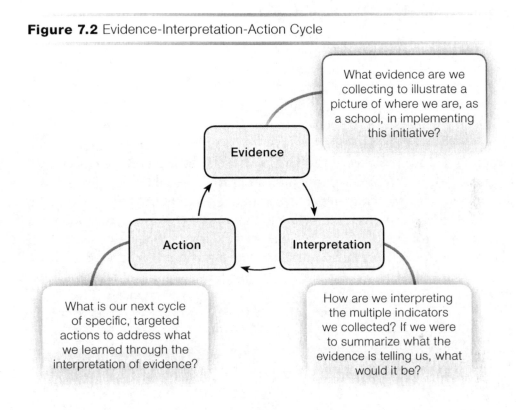

Consider this cycle brought to life by the example of Antonio Sarola, a principal, as he leads his elementary school toward lasting change.

Evidence: The collection of evidence is intended to provide information to the school leader about the success of the initiative. Gathered intentionally and strategically, the evidence matches the intended goal of the initiative in terms of the intended impact and the nature of the impact. For instance, consider the initiative of implementating a new set of rigorous national curriculum standards at an elementary school led by Principal Sarola. In its first year of implementation, it may be that one of the first actions he leads is professional development, intended to create new knowledge and awareness of the standards. If that is the goal for the initiative's strategy that first year, then the evidence that is collected must be in terms of teacher awareness and knowledge of the standards. Mr. Sarola then must make a decision as to how to collect that evidence in an efficient and useful way. Much more about evidence collection, the range of possible evidence, and the intended impact are developed later in this chapter.

Interpretation: The interpretation of the evidence collected after the standards professional development may be more important than the collection itself. In fact, the gathering of evidence is too often seen by school leaders as sufficient; however, no learning or significant action can result from the collection of the evidence unless it has been carefully interpreted by the maestro and his or her team. Thus, interpretation becomes the second part of the maestro's cycle. In essence, the question to be answered is, "What do those indicators we collected tell us? If we were to look at all of the measures we collected and summarize the result, what would it be?" To use our example again, we might assume that Principal Sarola determined to collect a short survey from teachers at the end of the two days of professional development that his teachers experienced at the beginning of the first year of implementation. He designed these statements and offered a Likert-type scale range of responses, from 1–5 (5 being the highest score). Principal Sarola decided that the survey would be given electronically to the teachers 24 hours after the conclusion of the last day of professional development. Figure 7.3 shows the individual responses from 27 elementary teachers and averages the scores (a simple mean), the statements, number of total responses, and mean scores.

Figure 7.3 Survey Data from the Standards Professional Development

Question:	Highly Disagree				Highly Agree	Avg.
	1	2	3	4	5	
	Frequency of Response					
I now have a much clearer overall understanding of the intent of the standards.	3	5	7	6	6	3.26
I have a greater awareness of the standards in my teaching area.	1	6	8	3	9	3.48
I feel confident to go back to my classroom and begin writing lesson plans using the standards as my guide.	7	7	8	3	2	2.48

The teacher responses tell Mr. Sarola something about the effectiveness of the training. You will recall that the purpose of the initial training was to create an awareness of the new standards and to begin to build knowledge with the teachers about the standards, and the few questions were directly related to those purposes. In interpreting the data, you may say that the professional development was moderately successful in that there were few responses to the first two items in the "1" or "highly disagree" response, yet the majority of the responses to the first two questions ranged from 1–3 on the Likert-type scale. Twelve of the teachers responded that they felt reasonably comfortable in their awareness of the standards in their teaching area, which was good news for Mr. Sarola. Dampening his enthusiasm, however, was that the great majority of teachers did not feel confident to go back to their classrooms and begin implementing plans using the standards.

To repeat, the interpretation of this evidence tells this school leader something and causes him to carefully consider his next actions to support the implementation of the standards. While not alarming or unpredictable, the information points Principal Sarola to the next set of carefully honed actions to support the teachers in their learning and eventual use of the standards.

Action: Completing the cycle of thinking is "action." The best actions are triggered by the careful interpretation of information, and signal that the school leader has carefully selected his or her next "moves" to support continuing change. In our example, the gathering of this information after the professional development training told this elementary school principal something and prompted him to carefully strategize his next supportive action. While the teachers appeared glad to participate in the professional development and seemed eager to learn more about the standards, they did not apparently walk away with a full understanding of the intent of the standards or the confidence to begin implementing lessons using the standards. While these responses might be predictable, they also point to how Principal Sarola can support the teachers, so they do begin to feel comfortable implementing the standards, which, of course, is the maestro's eventual intent. In interpreting the data, he determined that the teachers were hungry for more knowledge and understanding of the intent of the standards, and follow-up professional development was scheduled in October of the same year to deepen the teachers' understanding and to put teachers in their teams to begin to create lesson plans together that would incorporate one standard. Mr. Sarola concluded that this strategic action, on his part, would support the teachers in terms of moving the initiative forward.

Using Levels of Evaluation to Guide the Collection of Evidence

As stated earlier in this chapter, there are many considerations for contemplation before determining what evidence to collect to determine whether or not the initiative is working. Early in the initiative, the information gathered will be more in terms of the process, adult learning, and structural or organizational changes in the school to support the initiative. Later, when fully implementing the initiative and with the intent of examining real impact on students, other information will be more critical to the maestro. Five levels of evaluation originally proposed by Daniel Kirkpatrick (1959), and later by Thomas Guskey (2000), are useful frameworks for determining what evidence to collect as school staff members are getting deeper and deeper into the implementation of the changes. Again, it is useful to look at these levels of evaluation in terms of the life span of the initiative: Initiation, Implementation, or

Institutionalization. Evidence appropriate during the beginning stages of the initiative may not be suitable for later in the implementation phase. For more information about the stages of the life span of the initiative, refer back to Chapter Three. Review the levels of evaluation (Guskey 2000). The maestro will immediately determine that the levels shown in Figure 7.4 are hierarchical and more complex as you go deeper into them, requiring more time and resources.

Figure 7.4 Guskey's Levels of Evaluation for the Maestro

Evaluation Level	Goals for This Level	How Measured	Notes
Level One: How did participants react to the change or strategy?	Determining whether or not people liked the training or the change; do they feel that their time was well spent? how hopeful are they in terms of using the change?	The focus at this level is on the adults. Common measures are questionnaires, focus groups, surveys, interviews, and quick written statements.	This level is usually evaluated at the beginning of the initiative and is intended to improve the initial program design and/or delivery.
Level Two: Did participants acquire the knowledge and skill to begin to implement the initiative?	Determining to what extent the participants acquired the knowledge and skill to begin transitioning into implementation of the initiative	Again, the focus is on the adults who are learning what they need to implement the work. Common measures include participant written responses, pre/post assessments, etc.	This level is assessed because the leader understands that any initiative rests on whether or not the participants have learned enough to begin implementation.
Level Three: How has the school changed to support the initiative? Are structures, schedules, policies, or communication different because of the initiative?	Determining whether or not there are resources, structures, changes in communication that are directly intended to support the initiative	Common measures include school records, copies of minutes of meetings, policies or regulations, etc.	This is a shift to determine how the school has changed to advocate for the initiative and whether or not there are additional changes that must occur in the school to support the initiative's changes.

Evaluation Level	Goals for This Level	How Measured	Notes
Level Four: Are participants effectively and efficiently applying the new changes in their settings?	Shifting the focus of the evaluation from how the adults are responding to or learning about the initiative to whether or not school staff members are actually implementing the changes and the degree to which they are implementing the changes	Common measures include direct contact with teachers in the classrooms, questionnaires, examination of lesson plans, etc.	Level four marks the shift toward evidence to whether or not people are using the innovation and the changes. The focus is not yet on students but on application of practices.
Level Five: Are students benefiting from the changes in practice? What is the impact on their performance?	Trying to assess direct impact on students, their achievement, their emotional well-being, and their confidence	Typical measures include student records, student achievement data, results of informal student assessments, structured interviews with students, etc.	The purpose of this level is to determine the eventual impact on students and to give the school leader insight as to how to improve all aspects of program follow-up.

(Adapted from Guskey 2000)

Guskey reminds us that "evaluation at any of these five levels can be done well or poorly, convincingly, or laughably" (2000, 86). What is important to remember is that the information gathered at each level must be the *right* information to gather based on the goals for the initiative and how those goals are manifested in the yearly vision statements. One level is not more important than another; the importance in the level is its appropriateness for the current state of the initiative and the length of time the initiative has been in solid implementation. In addition, success at one of the first levels may be indicative of success later in the implementation, but that idea may not necessarily hold in all examples. Guskey (2000) notes that most initiatives and professional development strategies are only evaluated at the first level and never evaluated later on to determine if a) the professional development was ever implemented in classrooms and b) whether or not the professional development implementation had any impact on students at all.

A Critical Tool to Use Throughout the Initiative: The Stages of Concern

As teachers and staff members become more familiar with the initiative's changes and their impact on them, they experience a common set of developmental concerns. An examination of the concerns people have with the initiative is vital because teachers and staff members not only react intellectually to the demands of the change, but also personally and affectively. To put it another way, people experience a mix of "split personality" demands as they perceive their part in the change. On one hand, they experience all sorts of emotional and affective responses to the change, and these responses either hinder or accelerate their personal involvement in the change. On the other hand, people experience intellectual and logical demands of the change. They know, for example, that they are supposed to implement the change; they also learn about the changes and acquire the knowledge and skills to implement their perceived part of the change. As teachers and staff members work, then, in the school which is swirling with demands of high-impact changes, they are constantly bombarded with these feelings, emotions, and demanded behavior changes. Their personal, affective reactions to the changes can either derail their participation in the change, or if their reactions are supported and "facilitated" by the maestro, generally speaking, teachers and staff members will begin to implement the changes and their concerns will begin to shift from personal, more "selfish" concerns to concerns about implementing the changes correctly.

These concerns that staff members and teachers may have with the change have been researched for years in an affective dimension of the change process known as the Concerns Based Adoption Model (Hall and Hord 2010). The particular component of the Concerns Based Adoption Model (CBAM) that the maestro should review and use is the Stages of Concern. This component involves the assessing of concerns and gathering evidence of the concerns staff members have, providing valuable information to the leader in terms of how close teachers are to actually making changes in their classroom instruction to incorporate the changes of the initiative. In addition, it is just as important for school maestros to continue to use the Stages of Concern to assess concerns throughout the life span of the initiative, as concerns will change and if not addressed, could derail the initiative prematurely.

According to the developers of CBAM and the Stages of Concern, there are four different categories of concerns that include seven distinct stages. Figure 7.5 details the concerns that staff members and teachers typically have about an initiative.

Figure 7.5 The Stages of Concern

Category	Stage	Name of Stage	Description	Sounds Like
Impact	6	**Refocusing**	Teachers understand the broader benefits of the innovation and are interested in considering broad alterations or adaptations to make the initiative work even better.	"The (initiative) is working well. I think I have some ideas that would even make it better for our kids."
Impact	5	**Collaboration**	Teachers are interested and desire to work with others on the changes—sharing ideas and cooperating with others to make the impact on students even greater.	"Can our team work with the other teams on this? We have some ideas about how we are implementing the changes but want to hear from others about their perspectives."
Impact	4	**Consequence**	The teachers at this stage have shifted their concerns from management to students—they are now looking at how the initiative is affecting students, which students are affected by the changes, and what kinds of adaptations might be necessary.	"I can see the results now with my kids. I believe they are understanding mathematics better. I'm looking to see how I can tweak (the initiative) for them."

Category	Stage	Name of Stage	Description	Sounds Like
Task	3	**Management**	At this stage, teachers are more influenced by their concerns about "doing" the initiative—including the processes and tasks of actually implementing the first changes. The concerns are about time, efficiency, management, and scheduling.	"I can't seem to get all of it done in the time I have for mathematics. It's taking so long to write my lesson plans!"
Self	2	**Personal**	The concerns teachers have focus on the personal demands of the change and whether or not the individual feels adequate to take on the change. Concerns are about perceived rewards, conflicts, and decision making about the change.	"I look at all that is required of me and I have to wonder, where do I start? Can I do this? Is it worth it? Who decided that we had to do this?"
Self	1	**Informational**	Teachers want more information about the change. The concern is that they do not know enough detail about the components of the initiative and they desire to learn more about it and what is going to be demanded.	"I'm not sure I understand it. I'd like to learn more before I can commit to doing it."
Awareness	0	**Awareness**	There is little involvement with the initiative or little desire to learn more about it.	"This too will pass. This is another one of the district's big ideas that will fail."

(Adapted from Hall and Hord 2010)

The Value of the Stages of Concern for Evaluation of the Change

The assessment of concerns fits nicely within the Levels of Evaluation earlier developed in this chapter. Assessing reactions to the change (typically level one) can be manifested with the Stages of Concern. In fact, remember that the Stages of Concern can begin to tell the maestro how close he or she is to actual implementation of the initiative's changes, for the awareness and self categories of concerns are indicators that the teachers' most intense concerns are prior to actual implementation.

To put it another way, the concerns that teachers and staff members usually experience have nothing to do with students until the teachers and staff members are actually implementing the changes and experiencing management concerns. This is particularly worth noting for the maestro— indeed, many intense concerns teachers may have about the initiative will have little to do with the eventual impact (students, of course), and have much more to do with themselves! Typically, teachers experience informational and personal concerns early on in the life span of the initiative. These concerns are strong because they are at the core of each teacher's personal, emotional reaction to the change. If these concerns are not facilitated or addressed by the leader, the danger is that teachers will continue to experience concerns of this nature and never actually begin to implement the changes.

In addition, management concerns may be strong for teachers, as they indicate that the teachers are actually implementing the changes but experiencing concerns about that implementation. This is "good news, bad news" for the maestro, in that he or she can be gratified that the teachers are attempting to actually change their behaviors and implement the initiative in the classroom, but are having trouble with those changes. Again, if not facilitated or addressed, the maestro runs the risk of management concerns becoming so powerful that teachers begin to abandon the changes before ever assessing the impact the initiative has on students.

The Stages of Concern are "developmental" and indicate a typical progression through concerns, usually over time. It is important to note, however, that the process of concerns is not completely predictable. Concerns can change "on a dime," if circumstances within the school change, leadership changes, or other initiatives relegate the implemented initiative to a lesser place of importance.

Facilitating or Addressing the Stages of Concern

The Stages of Concern, then, provide a valuable tool for the gathering of evidence in terms of the way teachers are affectively reacting to the demands of the initiative. The tool is a useful one not only because it gives the maestro valuable and useful information; in addition, it is extremely easy to use in an ongoing, informal way. There are two ways of assessing concerns and gathering the useful evidence. They are the One-Legged Interview and the Open-Ended Statement (Hall and Hord 2010).

The One-Legged Interview

This is a short, oral, one-on-one interview conducted by the maestro, usually in an informal, but private, setting at school. The beauty of One-Legged Interviews is that multiple interviews can be conducted in any given school day, giving the maestro a "sampling" of the concerns that his or her teachers have at that point in time about the initiative. The maestro begins this interview by greeting the participant and asking him or her to narrow his thinking to the one initiative in question. Typically, the maestro provides a key question to trigger the participant's reactions and comments:

> *"When you think about your participation in (name the initiative), what are your concerns? What are you still worried about?"*

Once the question has been offered, the maestro must practice "responsive listening" by probing, and summarizing, but never solving or critiquing the participant's concerns at that time. In essence, the maestro is listening to all of the participant's responses, asking the participant to "tell me more" several times until he or she believes that the participant has told everything that is still concerning him or her. This One-Legged Interview usually ends with a thank you and the promise that the conversation has given the maestro valuable information that will help support the initiative even better. (Note that earlier in this explanation we are reminded not to try to fix or solve the concerns at that time—work in school coaching suggests that trying to fix or solve the concerns at that immediate time actually diminishes the participant, conveying the message that he or she cannot solve the problem by him or herself.)

When administering the One-Legged Interview to assess concerns, as stated before, the maestro can hold multiple interviews, in a given day, providing a wealth of information as to the way teachers are affectively responding to the initiative. Usually, these individual concerns will begin to fall into patterns, helping the maestro see how he or she might respond to the concerns that are most prevalent at the given time.

The Open-Ended Statement

The Open-Ended Statement is a written assessment of concerns and can be administered at one time to a large group of individuals or teachers. The essential question remains the same as in the One-Legged Interview; however, the question is posed or displayed and the participants are asked to respond in writing. These responses can then be collected and analyzed for patterns as well. One warning in conducting Open-Ended Statements is that participants, interestingly, may not feel as confident in writing their concerns as they do in speaking them. If the maestro uses the Open-Ended Statement as his or her tool in assessing concerns, the same assurances apply and should be stated to the participants—namely, that the participants should write about as many concerns as they are feeling and that their responses will not be used for evaluation purposes.

An Example of the Stages of Concerns in Practice

At this point in understanding the Stages of Concern, it is useful to see an actual example of how the Stages of Concern can provide valuable evaluation information for the maestro.

Dr. Benedict: A Case Study

At her particular high school, Dr. Benedict is guiding the teachers through their first year of learning about and implementing rigorous required state curriculum and learning standards. She knows that this is the first opportunity her teachers have this summer to review the principles undergirding the standards.

She enthusiastically embraces the summer professional development, and, as a part of her "Level One" evaluation (see the earlier Levels of Evaluation in this chapter), she determines to conduct several One-Legged Interviews after the summer professional development to determine the way teachers are reacting to the proposed changes of the standards. School starts for the year, teachers begin adjusting to their new students and curriculum, and Dr. Benedict decides that mid-October is the perfect time to conduct these One Legged Interviews.

One morning, in mid-October, Dr. Benedict spends time in the hallways and visits teachers' classrooms when students are not present. She manages to conduct ten randomly selected One-Legged Interviews, each lasting no more than two to three minutes in length. During every interview, she poses the same question:

"Think about our training in curriculum standards we learned about this summer and what you are doing to implement them. When you think about that, what are you still worried about? What are your concerns? Please tell me everything you are thinking."

As expected, Dr. Benedict gets an earful, and teachers seem pleased to have the chance to voice their concerns. She practices the basics of good questioning and does not attempt to solve their dilemmas; instead, she listens, probes, paraphrases, and thanks each teacher for trusting her and giving her such useful information. She does not write anything during each interview but jots down notes privately before she begins another one, forcing her to think about the overall most intense concern each teacher is relating to her. After the completed interviews, Dr. Benedict is happy to have gathered this evidence. She knows, however, that the real work is in interpreting what she has heard and determining whether or not any actions are required on her part. Figure 7.6 shows how the results of her interview were compiled.

Figure 7.6 Results of Dr. Benedict's Interviews

Teacher #	Major Concern	Notes
1	Awareness	Seemed unconcerned about the standards and didn't want any more information about it but didn't seem interested in learning more about it either
2	Informational	Didn't feel that she knew enough about it yet
3	Informational	Was confused about the standards and how it fit with her subject area—wanted to find out
4	Personal	Wasn't sure if it would be better than the way he taught and didn't like the fact that it was forced on him
5	Informational	Wanted to know more about it before she felt like she could begin to use it
6	Informational	Wanted to know more about it. Felt that the PD this summer was inadequate
7	Personal	Said that implementing it would take an incredible amount of time, and she wasn't sure if she was willing
8	Personal	Implementing it would be hard, and he wasn't sure if he could do it
9	Management	Was having a hard time writing lesson plans implementing it
10	Personal	Wasn't sure she could "pull it off"

Three months into the initiation of the rigorous standards, Dr. Benedict has valuable evidence as to the success of this major initiative. In interpreting the evidence gathered through her One-Legged Interviews, she finds that four of her teachers have intense Informational concerns; four of her teachers have intense Personal concerns; one teacher is attempting to implement the standards and having trouble; and one teacher just is not interested in the standards at all, probably believing that "this too shall pass." All in all, eight of the ten teachers expressed intense "self category" concerns (see Figure 7.6).

These interviews show predictable evidence. In fact, it is entirely reasonable that in the first few months of implementing the standards, teachers are actually not implementing them at all, but rather still studying and readying themselves for implementation through learning more about them and resolving personal concerns about the change to the standards. The important question for Dr. Benedict is "Do I do anything about what I learned?" If Dr. Benedict believes that these interviews demonstrated solid insights, she might develop additional training designed to provide more information to teachers about the curriculum standards and how teachers are implementing them. She could even consider smaller workshops or seminars where teachers began to work together on units of study infusing the standards-based changes into those units, demonstrating to teachers more practical knowledge of the standards and how it fits with their current teaching.

This example underscores the simple beauty of the "evidence-interpretation-action" cycle developed earlier in this chapter. The evidence that Dr. Benedict gathered was interpreted, and she felt that the interpretation propelled her to additional actions to foster the deeper investigation of the curriculum standards. Her actions are likely to be very beneficial to her teachers because they address the most intense concerns they had. Because their intense concerns were addressed, it is probable that the teachers were able to begin shifting their concerns away from themselves and toward "using the standards" or implementing it.

A Critical Tool When Checking for Implementation of the Initiative: The Levels of Use

As previously mentioned, the Stages of Concern tool is particularly useful at early stages of implementation, when the maestro is interested in determining how people are reacting to the change (the first level of evaluation). The tool is also considerably useful throughout the life span of the initiative, for the maestro's theory is that the concerns and the way people are reacting to the initiative will change over time as they become more comfortable with implementing the changes.

Another tool, the Levels of Use, provides incredibly valuable information for the maestro as he or she becomes more interested in how the changes are being *implemented* in the classrooms of the school. This tool does not focus on the affective reactions of the participants as much as how the participants' behaviors are changing in the classroom in relationship to the initiative's major changes. Essentially, the tool is based on years of research (Hall and Hord 2010). Hall and Hord's premise is that if the change maestro is interested in "determining whether a new approach is making a difference is to determine first if the innovation is being used" in the classroom at all and to what degree (81). In essence, there are levels in terms of how people act or behave with the innovation. In their work, Hall and Hord detail not only the levels, but operational definitions. Figure 7.7 is based on their work. Read each level from bottom to top, and think about the levels of use that you are seeing in your schools in terms of some initiative.

Figure 7.7 The Levels of Use

Category	Level	Name of Level	Description
Users of the Innovation	6	Renewal	Teachers are exploring or implementing some ways to either modify the innovation or make major changes in it, based on the results that they are getting from their students. They may be looking for additional materials or resources that will help them make the intended changes. They are self-directed to make the changes.
Users of the Innovation	5	Integration	Teachers are making adaptations for the benefit of students, but in concert with one or more teachers. They are seeking to collaboratively plan and hold each other accountable for the changes and are eager to share their results with each other.
Users of the Innovation	4b	Refinement	Teachers are beginning to see how well the innovation is working with their students. They are using assessments to make adaptation in the innovation to increase the benefits for the students.
Users of the Innovation	4a	Routine	Teachers have been given sufficient time and adequate help and are mastering the innovation and its use. Little adaptations are being planned—the goal, instead, is routine stabilization of the innovation.

Category	Level	Name of Level	Description
Users of the Innovation	3	Mechanical	Teachers are actively engaged with the innovation and are attempting to implement it routinely. There is an emphasis on short-term planning and improving the efficiency in using the innovation. The response of the teachers is more to the outside external mandate to use the innovation.
Nonusers of the Innovation	2	Preparation	Teachers have decided to use the innovation and are planning to intentionally begin implementing the changes.
Nonusers of the Innovation	1	Orientation	Teachers are learning more about the innovation, attending training, reviewing the texts, etc. There is no indication that the innovation is being used.
Nonusers of the Innovation	0	Nonuse	Teachers know very little about the innovation and exhibit no positive behavior toward using it. No action is being taken to implement the innovation.

(Adapted from Hall and Hord 2010)

Determining the Levels of Use at Schools

As stated before, the Levels of Use is vital in determining whether or not the innovation is being used, and to what degree of impact. The Stages of Concern may be assessed through either the One-Legged Interview or the Open-Ended Statement. The Levels of Use may be determined in one of two different ways—either by long-term observation or a carefully orchestrated conversation with individual teachers. If the maestro chooses the observation method, then he or she will look inside classrooms when the teacher is using the innovation and determine, over time, through several classroom visits, the level of use by that teacher. If this method is chosen, the maestro will want to target informal classroom visits to coincide with the use of the innovation and capture an array of visits over time with multiple teachers to determine the profile of how the innovation is being used at a certain point in time.

The other, more informal way to determine the Level of Use is for the maestro to visit, one-on-one, with the teacher in a "brief and casual way to gain a broad view of an individual's Level of Use in order to offer appropriate assistance" (Hall and Hord 2010, 87). While Hall and Hord originally suggested starting this conversation by asking, "Are you using the innovation?" it may be more productive and timely to ask, "How are you using this innovation in your classroom?" Asking *how* focuses the teacher on the positive assumption that he or she *is* using the innovation and encourages the teacher to describe the nature of that implementation operationally in his or her classroom. Depending on the answer to that beginning question, the maestro asks a series of additional questions to "stimulate the [teacher] to describe and provide examples of behaviors that he or she is taking in relation to the innovation" (Hall and Hord 2010, 87). The simple branch diagram in Figure 7.8 will assist the maestro in this quick, informal conversation. Notice the subsequent questions on either the "Yes, I'm using it" or "No, I'm not using it" branches.

Figure 7.8 Levels of Use

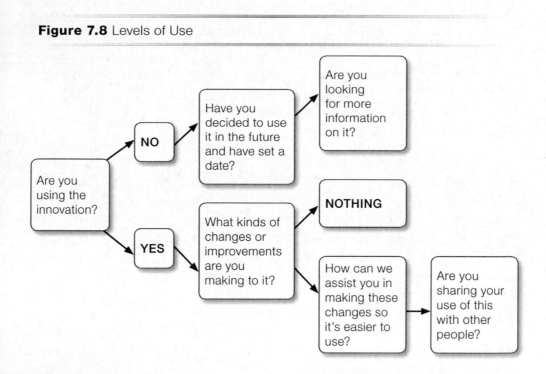

Thus, if a negative answer is first received, the maestro's job is to determine whether or not the teacher is "getting ready" to use the innovation or not at all. The subsequent questions help to determine the extent and amount of planning the teacher has done to "get ready" to use the innovation.

Conversely, if a positive answer is received, the maestro's responsibility is to determine whether or not the implementation is being done mechanically in the classroom (no changes, just following the script) to a more routine or refined implementation. The questions listed in this simple branch help illustrate the follow-up questions the maestro may use to determine the level of sophisticated implementation.

As in assessing the Stages of Concern, the informal interview is to be done in a non-evaluative way, in that the purpose of the interview is to gain this evidence of implementation and not to pass judgment on the teacher.

The Value of Assessing the Levels of Use

Just as the Stages of Concern gave valuable information in terms of how teachers were reacting to the innovation, the Levels of Use portrays a nice snapshot of how teachers are implementing the changes. Teachers' implementation of the innovation will often fall into patterns. These patterns of behaviors help the maestro understand where each teacher is in actualizing the changes and offers insights as to how the maestro can help support implementation of deeper, more refined changes.

There are danger points in determining the Levels of Use. For example, if the majority of teachers are mechanically implementing the change, this is cause for celebration but also a signal of trouble. If left to their own devices, more teachers will become frustrated with the changes as issues of time and management will overwhelm their good intentions; many teachers, then, will abandon the innovation altogether. Again, the maestro's job in the Evidence-Interpretation-Action cycle is to gather the evidence of implementation through the Levels of Use interview, compile all of the interviews, sense the patterns, and then interpret it in terms of his or her next actions to support it.

As you might expect, there is an interesting relationship between the concerns teachers may have (the affective responses to the innovation) and their behavior toward the innovation's changes (Levels of Use). Think about those changes using the information in Figure 7.9.

Figure 7.9 The Relationship Between Concerns and Behaviors

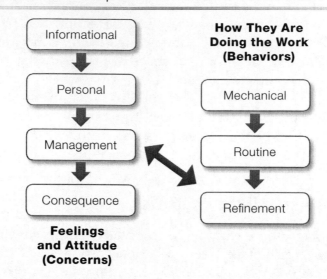

Note the relationship in Figure 7.9—when people are not interested in the change or seeing any information about the changes in the innovation, they are predictably in the "nonusers" levels. As stated before, when the individual makes the emotional commitment to begin using the innovation, they move into the "user" levels and quickly experience more operational difficulties, such as time, organization, and classroom management of the new system of learning. This typically coincides with the mechanical implementation, seen on the right side of this diagram. Therefore, gathering evidence from the Stages of Concern and Levels of Use gives the maestro two valuable pieces of evidence—one, detecting how people are emotionally and affectively responding to the change, and the other, detailing how people are actually implementing the changes. Two tools that assess two levels of evaluation, given repeatedly, gives the maestro two great forms of formative assessment that can help him or her alter his or her next actions.

Questions for Consideration and Discussion

1. What is your "cycle of work" at school? How does it compare with the Evidence-Interpretation-Activity cycle developed in this chapter? Why?

2. Are you regularly evaluating your most important initiatives? If so, at what levels are they being evaluated?

3. What concerns do teachers have about your most important initiatives? How do you know? Have their concerns changed over time?

4. How would you describe the level of implementation of your most important initiatives? How do you know?

5. If you were to make one change in how you evaluated your major programs, what would it be and why?

Chapter 8

Can I See an Example of This in Action?

At this point, an actual school-wide example might help us all see how all of the knowledge and skills on these pages can come to life in actual orchestrated practice. Read the following case study and contemplate the deliberations and actions by the leader to advance her initiative forward. While this example is not inclusive of all of the concepts in this book, it provides a realistic framework of how to layer in strategic support to help people not only embrace the necessary changes but put them into results-focused practice.

The Endeavor Elementary and Middle School: A Case Study

The First Year of Work

The Endeavor Elementary and Middle School, called EEMS from this point on, is a K–8 school in a suburban district with a diverse population of students. Several family languages other than English are spoken only in the homes, and the school rests in the middle of home and apartment complexes. Endeavor's principal, Serena Hodges, has been there for five years and enjoys favorable relationships with the teachers and parents of the students. She has involved her faculty for years in their own student data analysis. For at least four years, a major concern in this analysis has been the widening achievement gap among groups of students. These gaps appear in a variety of ways, including gaps among races of students, regular and special education students, and economically disadvantaged students and students of relative wealth.

Principal Hodges and the teachers have worked to close the gaps through individual effort and sporadic professional development, but to no lasting avail. Frustrated, Principal Hodges believes strongly that a school-wide focus on differentiated instruction might prove to be a pathway for differentiated practices, and resulting student achievement including the closing of achievement gaps. Instead of mandating this change, she begins discussing the idea with key teachers and teacher leaders and brings the idea up in faculty meetings. She also sends a group of teachers to a conference on differentiated instruction to determine their perspectives on such an initiative.

Principal Hodges is pleased to learn that, in all discussions and from feedback by the teachers attending the differentiation conference, there seems to be a consensus that a school-wide focus on differentiation would not only bring the school together but give teachers a common vocabulary and emphasis in the coming years. She feels that the time is right to begin working toward differentiated instruction as her major school initiative for the next few years.

She begins her orchestration with a more concerted effort to focus the conversation. In late April, after state-mandated testing, she begins her conversation at the faculty meeting and asks the teachers who attended the differentiation conference to begin a series of "sharing sessions" where they share what they learned at the conference and involve the other teachers in not only conversation but also practical analysis of the differentiation concepts in their own classrooms. This series of sharing sessions continues for three faculty meetings and concludes in late May.

Mrs. Hodges knows that the school is also in its third full year of implementation of a new set of standards and makes sure that teachers understand the connection between the standards and differentiated instruction. During these initial faculty meetings, teachers are asked to talk about the connections and work in small groups to talk about and list the ways that differentiation might help them implement the standards for deeper degrees of success.

In late May of this same year, Hodges wants to get a sense of how people are reacting to the proposed work in differentiated instruction. She believes that this change could be derailed by teachers' emotional responses to the idea; before she starts any work this summer, she wants to understand teachers' concerns about beginning this work in earnest.

At that last May faculty meeting, at the end of the teachers' sharing session, Principal Hodges asks teachers to take out a sheet of paper and fully answer this question: "When I think about beginning work in differentiated instruction, what are my concerns?" Teachers write their concerns and hand them in without signing the paper. This request serves as their "ticket out the door" at this faculty meeting. These open-ended statements will help Principal Hodges get the current perspectives held by her teachers.

See Chapter Three and how "coherence making" can assist people in making the change.

See Chapter Seven for the rationale behind asking for teachers' concerns about an initiative.

See Chapter Seven for information about how to conduct an open-ended statement.

These statements yield important information for Mrs. Hodges. At this point, teachers' concerns are predictably centering on the need for more information and concerns about how the effort will affect them personally in terms of time, reward, and whether or not they believe they have the knowledge and skill to implement differentiated instruction.

Mrs. Hodges believes that the first step in creating a differentiated school is to construct more knowledge about the concepts and skill in how to implement it. She believes that, because of the need to "send one message," training is the best model of professional development to begin this initiative. She creates a cadre of teachers who attended the differentiation conference and key central office personnel who have years of experience in differentiated instruction and charges them with conducting the differentiation training with the faculty. She utilizes the three summer professional development days to begin developing, through the training led by her cadre, a general understanding of differentiated instruction.

On the first day of summer training, Principal Hodges makes the results of her open-ended statement the previous May transparent to the participating teachers. She begins the day by sharing the results of these statements and breaking the teachers into groups to address their concerns. She talks realistically about these concerns and reminds her teachers that these concerns are predictable. This discussion serves as a springboard into the first day of training. Teachers seem pleased that Principal Hodges is being so open about the trials and tribulations of large-scale initiatives, and they appear to enthusiastically receive the training for the next three days.

> See Chapter Six to understand why Principal Hodges chose training as her model during the summer.

As an added evaluation measure, Principal Hodges believes that it is important at this point to determine teachers' reactions to and knowledge resulting from the training. At the end of each day, she asks teachers to respond to a simple prompt—one day, it is a ticket out the door; on the second day, it is a group response on chart paper. On the last summer training day, she requests that they respond to the training in terms of their "head, heart, and hands" (what they know now, how they feel about it, and what they will do with it).

> See Guskey's Levels of Evaluation (Levels One and Two) in Chapter Seven.

At the end of the third day, Mrs. Hodges makes the initiative clear in terms of expectations—she explains that they are in the "initiation" stage of the work and shares what she expects during this phase in terms of teacher learning and action. She encourages the teachers to continue to study and talk about differentiated instruction and to begin to try out "low-prep" strategies they've heard about that seem simple to implement.

> Chapter Six explains the initiation phase of the work.

School starts in the early fall, and Mrs. Hodges continues supporting teachers through her conversations with them, asking them not only to keep thinking about their training but also how they see themselves beginning to implement anything they had learned. These conversations are intended to build the relationship and focus on the work, gently pressing for each teacher to begin making small changes that they feel they can easily implement. Principal Hodges stresses that they are still in the initiation phase and that part of the changes are to begin thinking about implications for each one of them and how they see themselves in differentiated instruction.

> See Chapter Six for the three goals of successful conversations.

She continues to encourage teams of teachers to openly discuss differentiated strategies and to share these strategies with each other. She uses the "trust facets" to frame her conversations with teams, attempting to create even deeper levels of trust among teachers, so they will feel more and more comfortable sharing their successes and failures with each other.

> See Chapter Five for a reminder on the trust facets.

In October, after several weeks of supportive, informal conversations with teachers, about differentiated instruction, Mrs. Hodges asks for volunteers from her teachers to create a vision for differentiated instruction. She attempts to create a balanced committee, representing all aspects of her school staff. In mid-October, she convenes the group for several afternoons as they craft a vision. The completed statement is almost a page long and is a carefully articulated word description of what they hope to achieve when differentiated instruction is fully institutionalized at Endeavor Elementary and Middle School. The vision gives guidance in four areas: a) what teachers are doing, b) what students are doing, c) how the school is structured, and d) how leadership is functioning—all when the vision is fully realized.

Chapter Four gives specific guidance on how to craft a vision for the initiative.

This vision is shared with all faculty members in late October at a brief faculty meeting, and all staff members are asked to react to the vision as they work in small groups. They deliberate and list potential roadblocks to the vision. These lists are given to Mrs. Hodges for her consideration and management.

In early November, Principal Hodges again asks for volunteers among her staff. At this time, the new volunteer committee will convene and write a "first-year" vision that will guide the work for the first full year of implementation (this entire school year and into the next summer) and align with the overall vision. Again, the group creates a simple one-year vision and the critical steps that must be accomplished for the remainder of the year in order for them to realize this first-year vision. These documents are shared with teachers at the faculty meeting before Thanksgiving. At that meeting, Mrs. Hodges creates a bit of "heat" for the teachers, using the documents to outline practical expectations for the rest of the year.

Chapter Four also gives instructions on how to develop a yearly vision for each year of support. See Chapter Three for a description of "heat and light."

The winter holidays provide a natural break to the implementation of differentiated instruction. Teachers and students return in January, and Mrs. Hodges believes that they are ready to begin implementing varieties of grouping strategies (outlined in the first-year vision as one of the major areas of emphasis). Early in the month, she begins communicating this idea in her informal conversations, using the conversation framework to focus on small grouping strategies. From these conversations, she elicits individual goals from each teacher in terms of his or her implementation of small grouping strategies. Principal Hodges concludes these conversations with a commitment to look for signs of these grouping strategies when she visits the classrooms in the spring.

From January until April, Principal Hodges conducts her usual classroom walk-throughs and mandated formal observations, and she uses these insights to continue to focus on the one-year vision, and more specifically,

See Chapter Five for the conversation framework.

the small successes teachers are having in experimenting with small group strategies. During these conversations, she asks about the results teachers are seeing in terms of students. Examples of questions she uses are "What was the effect on your students?" and "How do you know your students benefited from this grouping strategy?" At all times, she acknowledges the efforts and points out the successes teachers are having.

Two of the teachers appear resistant to using any of the grouping strategies. Principal Hodges spends time with these two teachers, using the forms of resistance and the resistance formula to better diagnose the teachers' reasons behind the resistance. She continues her conversations with these two teachers, using the vision to continually focus their work and gain their commitment to trying grouping strategies with their students before the end of the school year. She applies "heat" to each one of them, reminding them that implementing small grouping strategies is nonnegotiable.

Chapter Five contains the forms of resistance and the resistance formula.

In February, Principal Hodges decides to determine the extent of implementation of the grouping strategies, using the Levels of

Use. In her formal and informal observations, she looks for varying degrees of sophistication of grouping strategies. She hypothesizes that most teachers will be in the orientation, preparation, or mechanical level of implementation, and she either uses her observation data or one-on-one conversations with teachers to determine overall levels of behavior toward implementing the grouping strategies. From these observations and conversations, she creates a "profile" of the most frequently occurring levels of use in order to determine any actions she should take to support the teachers.

Principal Hodges determines that most of her teachers are in the early mechanical stages of implementation of differentiated grouping strategies. The source of the issue with their mechanical implementation seems to be managing the different groups of students and their differentiated materials while minimizing classroom disruptions and lost instructional time.

See Chapter Seven for the Levels of Use and how to determine the patterns for the levels at a school.

Therefore, in early March, Mrs. Hodges announces informal, optional afternoon practical sessions at her school, facilitated by members of the original training cadre, so teachers can address their management and mechanical issues in an atmosphere of low-risk and collegial support. She knows that at this point, more training is not what is needed; as teachers move into more and more implementation of their ideas, her professional development needs to shift into more practical, job-embedded forms of support for classroom practice.

Mrs. Hodges also knows that as she is pressing for implementation, teachers' concerns have probably changed. She conducts informal One-Legged Interviews in the month of March to determine if the concerns have shifted from informational and personal to different stages. Indeed, the overwhelming

See Chapter Six for more information about job-embedded professional development.

concerns at this point in the year are management concerns, supporting the idea that they are now implementing grouping strategies and are having various issues with this first step in changing practice. She is pleased that she has initiated the job-embedded, collegial, practical sessions this spring and commits to continuing them for the rest of the school year as needed.

In the late spring, Principal Hodges reconvenes the original one-year vision writing committee. During this meeting, she shares the Gradual Release of Responsibility model with them, asking each member to speculate on "next steps" to move the teachers toward more responsibility model for deep implementation of grouping strategies and the other concepts in differentiated instruction. They brainstorm ideas to move teachers into deeper responsibility, generating a proposed set of "next steps" for the second-year vision. Principal Hodges regards these ideas as a draft, for further development during the summer.

> Chapter Seven gives specific information about conducting One-Legged Interviews.

For the rest of the school year, Mrs. Hodges supports the implementation of grouping strategies, holds conversations with teachers about it, and listens to any concerns that are generated. At the end of the school year, when celebrating successes, she points intentionally to the teachers' efforts in implementing one aspect of differentiated instruction this year. She reminds them that their implementation of grouping strategies has become the "new norm" for the school and restates that small grouping strategies are to be a part of every teacher's repertoire from now on. Mrs. Hodges also reviews the one-year vision and gives her perspective about their accomplishments. She reviews the second-year ideas the committee has drafted and breaks the teachers into small groups, asking them to respond to the ideas and generate their own. All of these documents

> Chapter Five contains a detailed description of the Gradual Release of Responsibility model.

are collected at the end of the meeting and used by Principal Hodges for her reflection as the school year closes.

A Summary of the Second Year of Work

At Endeavor, the second year of work toward differentiated instruction really continues the first full year of actual implementation (since part of the first year at the school was initiating the idea and building the momentum toward beginning training and action). Mrs. Hodges knows that these elements are critical to her success and must be considered and planned for second-year orchestration.

A second-year vision must be crafted as the guiding document for year two. The second-year vision must be developed from the notes and thoughts generated in mid and late spring of the previous year. This second-year vision must drive the work now, and the second-year vision should build on the first-year statement and lead toward the full vision crafted at the beginning of the first year.

Teachers may need additional training during the second year; however, they will also need more practical, informal, collegial forms of professional development that are geared toward problem solving and actual implementation and analysis of practices. These professional-development opportunities must be dispersed throughout the second year instead of front-loading all of them in the summer before the second year.

Teachers' concerns will change during the second year. Mrs. Hodges must assess these concerns periodically and act on them.

As more differentiated practices are assumed, teachers' levels of use of them will vary. Mrs. Hodges must continue to focus on a refined use of all practices for real student outcomes, and hold conversations with teachers to help them continue to analyze and alter their practices for deeper and more profound impact.

Principal Hodges knows that for year two, she will be looking at the application of learning (Guskey's fourth level of evaluation). She also knows that she may begin to look at student outcomes and achievement in both formal and informal forms.

Thoughts about Years Three and Beyond

Principal Hodges remembers that every year calls for a "reset" in terms of where the faculty is in learning about and implementing more and more sophisticated differentiated practices. She uses what she knows about professional development, the Gradual Release of Responsibility model, vision statements, conversations, and evaluation methods to continue to get a clearer picture of what implementation looks like at Endeavor Elementary and Middle School.

Beginning in year three, she expects the level of use of strategies to have moved toward routine and refined use. She uses what she knows about the levels of evaluation to begin regularly looking at student achievement to determine the amount of gains groups of students are making to close achievement gaps.

Where Does the Maestro Start?

At schools, we are often caught up with the pressing tasks of our daily leadership. Orchestration, like the great conductors generating great music, requires us to consider the big sounds and the big ideas of our work and focus less on the day-to-day tasks that, in fact, detract us from our goals. Strategic in nature, orchestration requires us to look at our initiatives as "living things," in need of nourishment along the way and changes in our practices to continue to support the living changes as they develop, grow, and mature. It requires us to work with people in different ways—not like vessels to be filled but partners in the change. This partnership holds us all more accountable and responsible, for it is in this organizational loyalty that the changes will ignite and hold. Orchestration requires us to plan adult learning and to evaluate progress in ways that listen to the concerns of others and describe the changes that are happening. And finally, orchestration requires a nimbleness and flexibility in the leader. In thinking about your first steps toward orchestration, remember first that you can do it! Secondly, consider these questions as you begin the development of a more melodic development of changes at your school.

Questions for Consideration and Discussion

1. What is the initiative that has the most promise for lasting impact at your school?

2. What can you do to "ready" the school and staff for the change?

3. How will you design the life span of the change?

4. Who will you involve in orchestrating the changes?

5. How should the changes look different over time?

6. How will you use the vision to drive and evaluate the changes?

7. How do you like to work with people and how will this influence the kinds of conversations you have with them about the change?

8. How will you manage the changes over time so the momentum is sustained?

References Cited

Brophy, Jere E. 2010. *Motivating Students to Learn*. New York, NY: Routledge.

Deal, Terrence, and Kent Peterson. 2000. *The Leadership Paradox: Balancing Logic and Artistry in Schools*. San Francisco, CA: Jossey-Bass.

DuFour, Richard, Rebecca DuFour, and Robert Eaker. 2008. *Revisiting Professional Learning Communities at Work: New Insights for Improving Schools*. Bloomington, IN: Solution Tree.

Fullan, Michael. 2001. *Leading in a Culture of Change*. San Francisco, CA: Jossey-Bass.

———. 2007. *The New Meaning of Educational Change (4th Edition)*. New York, NY: Teachers College Press.

Gallagher, Robert. 2005. "The Change Formula." Congregational Development. Accessed on February 28, 2014. http://www.congregationaldevelopment.com/storage/Change%20formula.pdf.

Gordon, Stephen P. 2004. *Professional Development for School Improvement: Empowering Learning Communities*. Upper Saddle River, NJ: Pearson.

Gulamhussein, Allison. 2013. "Teaching the Teacher: Effective Professional Development in an Era of High Stakes Accountability." Alexandria, VA: The Center for Public Education

Guskey, Thomas R. 2000. *Evaluating Professional Development*. Thousand Oaks, CA: Corwin Press.

Hall, Gene H., and Shirley M. Hord. 2010. *Implementing Change*. Upper Saddle River, NJ: Pearson.

Joyce, Bruce, and Emily Calhoun. 2010. *Models of Professional Development: A Celebration of Educators*. Thousand Oaks, CA: Corwin Press.

Killion, Joellen, Cindy Harrison, Chris Bryan, and Heather Clifton. 2012. *Coaching Matters*. Oxford, OH: Learning Forward.

Kirkpatrick, D.L. 1959. Techniques for evaluating training programs. A four-part series beginning in Nov. issue vol 13, No 11 of Training and Development Journal (then titled Journal for the American Society of Training Directors).

Kise, Jane G. 2006. *Differentiated Coaching: A Framework for Helping Teachers Change*. Newbury Park, CA: Corwin Press.

Learning Forward. 2011. Oxford, OH. Standards for Professional Learning.

Lewin, Roger, and Birute Regine. 2000. *The Soul at Work: Unleashing the Power of Complexity Science for Business Success*. New York, NY: Simon and Schuster.

Love, Nancy. 2009. *Using Data to Improve Learning for All: A Collaborative Inquiry Approach*. Thousand Oaks, CA: Corwin Press.

Patterson, Kerry, Joseph Grenny, Ron McMillan, and Al Switzler. 2002. *Crucial Conversations: Tools for Talking When Stakes are High*. New York, NY: McGraw-Hill.

Pearson, David, and Margaret C. Gallagher. 1983. "The Gradual Release of Responsibility Model of Instruction." *Contemporary Educational Psychology* 8: 112–123.

Pink, Daniel H. 2009. *Drive: The Surprising Truth About What Motivates Us*. New York, NY: Riverhead Books.

Quinn, Robert E. 1996. *Deep Change: Discovering the Leader Within*. San Francisco, CA: Jossey-Bass.

Senge, Peter M. 1999. *The Dance of Change: The Challenges to Sustaining Momentum in a Learning Organization*. New York, NY: Doubleday.

Tschannen-Moran, Bob, and Megan Tschannen-Moran. 2010. *Evocative Coaching: Transforming Schools One Conversation at a Time*. San Francisco, CA: Jossey-Bass.

Tschannen-Moran, Megan. 2004. *Trust Matters: Leadership for Successful Schools*. San Francisco, CA: Jossey-Bass.

Walsh, Jackie Acree, and Beth Dankert Sattes. 2010. *Leading Through Quality Questioning: Creating Capacity, Commitment, and Community*. Thousand Oaks, CA: Corwin Press.

Wiggins, Grant, and Jay McTighe. 2007. *Schooling by Design: Mission, Action, and Achievement*. Alexandria, VA: ASCD.

Quick Resources and Tools

The resources contained in this section are intended to be used as a quick reference tool for the essential ideas found in this book.

Orchestration: The School Leader's Framework

These key concepts form the foundation for this book and the key elements for the leader to consider as he or she develops differentiated strategies for working with the adults in the school. For more information, please see Chapter Two and Figure 2.3.

Quick Resources and Tools *(cont.)*

My Orchestration Log

This log is intended to help the leader record major conversations and actions. Analysis of the log can show patterns in behavior and tone. For more information, please see Chapter Two and Figure 2.4.

Contact	Nature of the Conversation or Action	Telling?	Some Telling?	Consulting?	Consulting and a Little Coaching?	Coaching?

Quick Resources and Tools *(cont.)*

The Life Span of a School Initiative

According to research, there are three distinct, developmental phases to the change process. Understanding these phases is key to the success of an initiative. The phases are summarized in the diagram below. For more information, please see Chapter Four and Figure 4.2

Initiation
- The initial planning for the initiative
- The "first steps" in readying for the initiative
- The initial training or professional development

Implementation
- The initial use of the initiative
- The support for the first experiences
- The push from "learning about it" to "using it"

Institutionalization
- The initiative becomes a part of the culture of the school
- Ongoing support and troubleshooting to keep the initiative successful

Quick Resources and Tools *(cont.)*

The Gradual Release of Responsibility Model

Although originally used to frame the gradual release of learning from a teacher to a student, the concepts in this model can guide school leaders as they develop and encourage staff members to implement changes. For more information, please see Chapter Five and Figure 5.8.

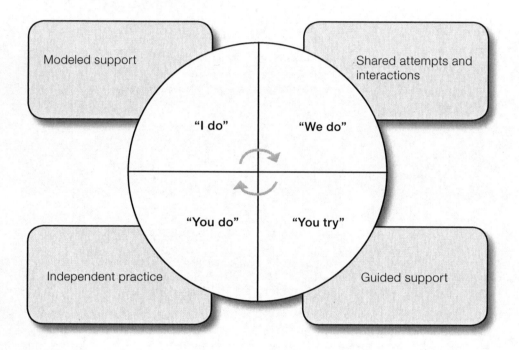

Quick Resources and Tools (cont.)

The Leader's Conversation Framework

This framework can be used as a guide and preparation tool when planning specific conversations with others as relevant to the initiative being implemented, in order to help ensure that the conversation is productive and the necessary outcomes are reached. For more information, please see Chapter Five and Figure 5.10.

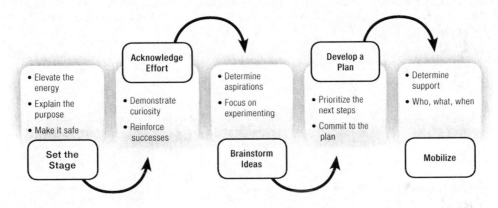

Quick Resources and Tools *(cont.)*

Several Effective Professional Development Designs

This chart can be used to support the planning of professional development that is best suited for the initiative at the particular time of the initiative's life span. For more information, please see Chapter Six and Figure 6.5.

Professional Development Design	Description	Factors to Consider
Training, Courses, Seminars	Highly structured PD far removed from the classroom context, selected when it is determined that a large number of staff members need to learn from an "expert" to quickly gain knowledge or awareness.	• The urgency of the change and necessity of quick acquisition of knowledge and/or awareness • The need for application of practice • Training is not necessarily linked to actual application of practice • The plan to support the application of practice after the training
Immersion	An inquiry-based design in which teachers are "immersed" in the activities they would be asking students to fulfill. Typically, immersion is accomplished at schools where teachers work through materials, kits, and textbooks together, creating and experiencing the same kinds of assignments and activities they will ask students to perform. Immersion is useful for gaining knowledge, awareness, and providing reflection time.	• Time for teacher collaboration and practice • The commitment teachers have to application • Trust among the teachers • Support for resources to focus the immersion
Curriculum Development and Implementation	Teachers working together to either develop new lesson plans or strengthen/revise previous practice. Curriculum development is useful for developing new knowledge about a content area and providing practice for implementation of the new plans within a collegial setting.	• Time for curriculum development, discussion, and implementation • Ongoing support for application • Trust and history of communication and dialogue among the practicing teachers • The extent of problem solving that teachers must accomplish and the practicality of their demands
Analyzing Student Work	Examining samples of student work and products in order to understand students' thinking and learning strategies around an idea or concept. The study of the work leads to further decisions about appropriate teaching strategies, re-teaching, and materials selection. Design is particularly effective in supporting reflection, new knowledge, and awareness.	• Commitment to a unified assignment and the selection of work samples to review • Trust and history of communication and commitment to experimenting with new strategies • Time for review and conversation • Whether or not the initiative is in full implementation

Quick Resources and Tools *(cont.)*

Several Effective Professional Development Designs *(cont.)*

Professional Development Design	Description	Factors to Consider
Case Analyses	Case analyses can include case studies, video clips, etc. The examination presents a real-life scenario in which teacher practice is discussed and deliberated, with implications in terms of issues or outcomes. Case analyses are effective for reflection and the acquisition of knowledge.	• Materials and resources for cases • Time for extended review and conversations • Trust and history of communication skills among the participating teachers
Mentoring and Coaching	Usually one-on-one with equally or sometimes more experienced teacher to improve teaching and learning through feedback, observation and conversation, problem solving, and/or co-planning. Mentoring and coaching are particularly effective when the goal includes practice, knowledge, and/or reflection.	• Human resources • The levels of trust throughout the organization • A history of conversation and problem solving • Peer-to-peer collaboration and comfort
Study Groups and Book Studies	Related study groups and book studies involve small groups in regular, structured, and collaborative interactions regarding topics identified by the group and/or by the book/resource being used. Book studies are particularly useful for awareness and knowledge. Study groups have a bias toward implementation of new practice after the learning; therefore, they are useful if the goal for professional development includes knowledge, awareness, practice, and/ or reflection.	• Fiscal resources for the materials to be examined and studied • Time for study and collaboration • Trust among staff members • History of peer-to-peer work
Action Research	A close cousin to study groups and book studies, action research is known by many titles. Disciplined action research involves locating a problem area in student learning, collecting data about the problem, studying relevant resources, deciding to take action, and then studying the results in terms of future action or decision making. Action research is particularly useful for knowledge, practice, and reflection.	• History of peer-to-peer work • Trust among sharing of practice • Time for study and collaboration • Relevant when the initiative is in full implementation

Quick Resources and Tools *(cont.)*

Evidence–Interpretation–Action Cycle

Leaders must incorporate this cycle as they evaluate the progress of an initiative and consider new actions to support the work as it develops in deeper ways during implementation. For more information, please see Chapter Seven and Figure 7.2.

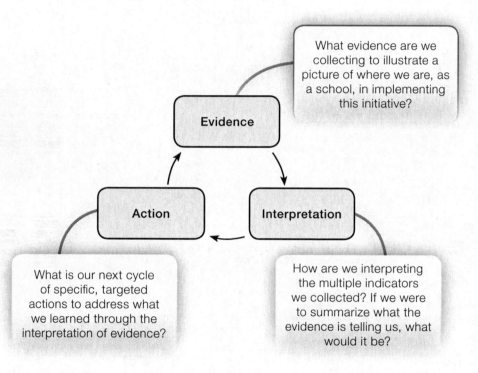